CATALYSIS

CATALYSIS
A Recipe to Slow Down or Abort Humankind's Leap to War

ALICE LOMBARDO MAHER, M.D.

International Psychoanalytic Books (IPBooks)
New York • http://www.IPBooks.net

International Psychoanalytic Books (IPBooks)
Queens, NY
Online at: http://www.IPBooks.net

Printed in the United States of America

Paperback ISBN: 978-1-7320533-9-7

Acknowledgements

If it takes a village to raise a child, I'm fortunate to have co-created an extraordinary Facebook village. My friends provide me with the perfect combination of friendship, education, nurturing and challenge. This book could not have been written without them. A partial list includes:

Ron Allen, Jessica Arenella, Kyle Arnold, Goran N. Arsov, Hans Bakker, Hank Benson, Pat Bracone, Sean Campbell, Rick Chaney, Jeff Cole, Shivakami Steve Corbett, Howard Covitz, Mukta Agrawal Daga, Jacqueline Damian, Shlomo Dror, Linda Olsen Fitak, John Foy, Jeanne Friedland, Neil R. Friedman, Joseph Gardella, Jean Garrett-Franken, Sara Goldberg, Zach Goldberg, Stephen Greenberg, Ruth Gwynne-Karlin, Fred Henry III, Donna Hortz, Justin Hortz, Liz Howie, Gordon Howie, Anna Klambauer, Ruth Elliott Klein, Bill Lawrence, Judy Logue, Greg Lupion, Michael Mantas, John Mason, Kevin Matthews, Rehana Matri, James McGrath, Bill Miessner, Patricia Leonforte Minerva, Kevin Moore, Helen Muhlbauer, Tyra Nasrin, Kari Ann Owen, Helen Petras, Laurie O'Dowd Piccinni, Michael Piccinni, Arnold Richards,

Maryann Parente Riordan, Kathie Rudy, David Salvage, Laura Schultz, Robert Shanbaum, Neva Shaw, Diantha Day Sprouse, Pamela K. Taylor. Banu İbaoğlu Vaughn, Tom Vogler, Paul Wadey, Heward Wilkinson and Nick Wood

Kevin Moore, Mukta Agrawal Daga, Banu Vaughn, Anna Klambauer and Shivakami Steve Corbett did, or imagined doing, their own dialogue projects. They wrote about their experiences beautifully.

Peggy and Tony Lombardo, Jim Maher, and James and Robert Maher taught me about different forms of love, boundaries and separateness, communication across divides, and the dimension of time. Despite many weekends watching me write passionate theoretical/philosophical letters and talk about a vision of changing the world, my sons turned into amazing young men anyway. The cover is a photo by Jimmy, a photographer, and the word "recipe" in the title is a nod to Bobby, a chef. None of us would be where we are without Mary Togher, who helped raise them.

Many others offered concrete help as I struggled to transform imaginary shapes into solid form. Lois Oppenheim shared my vision of changing society's perspective on mental illness. Without her as co-creator, our mental health documentaries and The Hot Stove Project would never have come into existence. The enormously talented Sheryll Franko, Sean Campbell, and Ben Wolf did the hard work of writing, directing and editing those films.

John Foy helped me set up my non-profit organization and introduced me to the Street Squash afterschool program and to students and faculty at Hunter College High School. There I met the amazing people who helped me develop and implement Emotional Imprint pilot projects. Melissa Brand designed the curricula and Sasha Diamond-Lenow taught them brilliantly. Sasha helped develop the internship program, and the Street Squash interns worked with Kaley Pillinger and Sydney Allard from Hunter to create and edit the *Divides* eBook.

Divides is based on the work of Dr. Vamik Volkan. I'm very grateful to him and to Lord John Alderdice, for their willingness to meet with our students and nurture their interest in psychoanalytic perspectives on large group conflict.

Susan Dansker, Jonathan and Matthew Bogaty, and Andrew Wiese made my visions come alive in their elegant design, programming and editing of the COC, EI, *Divides* and HSP websites. Susan's friendship, the perfect combination of support and challenge, remains invaluable.

Thanks to Arnie Richards for fighting with me for decades, staying in the ring despite some difficult moments, always remaining my friend and now publishing my book.

Bernice Arricale has been my best friend and muse since we met in the first grade at Most Holy Redeemer. For the last 60 years, she used her superpower to help me keep my head in the air and my feet on the ground. My relationship with the extraordinary Dr. X was modeled, at least in part, on my relationship with her.

I'm good at seeing big pictures, but attention to detail is another matter. My terrific editor, Carol Skolnick, not only corrected my typos and sentence structure; she helped me see my words through the eyes of a curious but neutral reader.

Finally, thanks to Dr. X. I'm enormously grateful for the risk he was willing to take to nurture a young woman with a strange vision and an even stranger request. I hope and expect that the world will come to know his name, study what he did and imitate it for future generations.

Those generations will include my new grandson, Avery. As of this writing, he is just a few weeks old, but already he is a unique and wonderful person. He represents for me all of the children for whom I have written this book…who will take these ideas, make them their own and change the world. Avery, this book is for you.

Table of Contents

Section III: The Problem of War

Section IV: The Origins

Introduction

I set myself a very hard task. In this short book, I will present what I believe to be a major paradigm shift in human understanding and discourse. My goal is to intrigue you, coax you to think and behave in new ways, and convince you to become part of a movement.

This movement will lead to:

1) a new way of communicating across human divides

2) a new language to codify that process

3) a different education for our children

4) creative solutions to intractable conflicts

5) the ability to slow down or abort humankind's leap to war

6) a shift in the direction of human consciousness and evolution

7) an exciting, challenging and rewarding adventure into unknown territories

If you're going to consider my idea, you'll need to imagine this possibility: *the next leap in the evolution of our species will happen with conscious understanding and conscious intent, as a new language for communication across human divides emerges.*

I will present a theoretical model, one that integrates and reframes models from disparate fields. I will tell you about some simple pilot projects, and I will share concrete suggestions for ways that everyone can begin to implement these ideas in the here and now.

Ideas as big as this one don't emerge out of thin air. In the final chapter, I will describe the personal trajectory that led to my conclusions and to my absolute conviction about them.

Changing Our Consciousness

1

Human Bridges, Creative Solutions to Conflict and Worthy Leaders: Are They Possible?

Our species is brilliant at bridging divides in the scientific and technological arenas. We build spaceships that fly to other planets. We pick up the phone in one country and speak to someone in another. Malignancies deep inside our bodies are cured with targeted treatments. When problems arise, we tackle them until they're solved.

In most fields, the best and most accurate eventually rise to the top. The best athletes train for a long time to win gold, while competitors mourn the loss and work harder to win the next round. The best scientists get the grants and design the studies that give birth to new paradigms. The best technological innovations are designed by the best teams. The best weapon systems are adopted and, unfortunately, used.

In those arenas, conflict, paradox and error stimulate curiosity. Hypotheses arise, experiments are designed, mistakes are accepted. After considerable struggle, new insights leading to creative solutions emerge. In *The Structure of Scientific Revolutions* (1962), Thomas Kuhn demonstrates how major paradigm shifts occur in response to the emergence of anomalies.[1]

In the human arena, the opposite is true. Our species has not yet developed the capacity to bridge psychological divides, solve human problems and shift human paradigms. We're not excited by contradictions. We don't embrace anomalies and work to resolve conflicts in ways that allow new insights to emerge and be adopted.

In the human arena, conflict and paradox lead to interminable argument, ridicule, pre-judgment and rejection. The best people often don't rise to the surface and lead, while the ones who do can be severely compromised by the forces that brought them there. We enjoy finding flaws in our leaders and ripping them to shreds.

God/"God" seems both essential and non-existent. But rather than explore that fascinating paradox we choose to fight against or flee from those who think differently.

If you believe something that contradicts what I believe—if you're liberal and I'm conservative, if you're religious and I'm atheist, if you see the world from a vantage point that seems wrong to me—a typical response is that you must be stupid, crazy, uninformed, prejudiced or evil. You threaten me so I have to avoid you, make you stop or make you go away.

Often we construct simplistic and unstable bridges by saying, *I'm okay; you're okay. We're all more human than otherwise, and*

---

1 Kuhn, Thomas (1962). *The Structure of Scientific Revolutions.* University of Chicago Press. Kuhn's landmark book challenged the idea of "normal science," arguing that progress is not always rational and logical; sometimes it's the result of a revolutionary shake-up.

our beliefs must be equally worthy of attention and respect. Truth and reality are relative anyway. If your opinion is that the sky is green, then it's green for you and that's fine. Children are taught to have opinions before they understand what they're talking about and well-argued opinions are accepted as equally valid.

We share almost everything in our global economy and social media. But we lack a shared moral compass and a shared search for truth.

We can't teach our children ways to search for and discover human truths and live by them, because we don't know what Truth is or how to open up pathways to reach for it.

Few sturdy structures exist to resolve human conflict and bridge human divides. Religious and political ideologies seem as if they always were and always will be. We fight over them and we divide into subgroups, but we don't know how to incorporate new information without losing the essence of cherished belief systems that may contribute significantly to our individual and group identities.

This phenomenon is NOT anyone's fault. Entrenched beliefs have been shown to be hard-wired and rarely amenable to change, even when facts demonstrate the opposite of what we're inclined to believe. All of us can read the same books about Karl Marx, Sigmund Freud or Jesus Christ. If we're inclined to believe their models, we will believe, and if we're inclined to scoff at them, we will scoff. Additional information makes little difference.

This phenomenon may not be our fault, but it's definitely our problem. It's a problem we have the capacity to solve. If we can put a man on the moon, we can solve this problem too.

2

Accepting Our Own Nature:
The Beginning of a Solution

We put a man on the moon because Isaac Newton (as my reinvented fable goes) sat under an apple tree. An apple fell on his head and instead of cursing and yelling, *Ouch! Bad apple!* he thought, *Eureka! There's an unseen force that pulled that apple to the ground! Let's call it "gravity" and figure out how it works!*

In the human arena, "bad apples" fall on us all the time. What do we typically do? We yell, *Ouch! Bad apple! You have to stop behaving like that right now! I'm going to post a meme about how wormy and moldy you are!*

I'm going to do something analogous to what Newton did. I'm going to help you understand that there are forces of human nature that simply ARE. Once we accept that there are certain dynamic forces in all of us that represent fundamental building blocks of our species, we'll stop criticizing each other and admonishing each other to be different.

Once we overcome that serious but easily addressed obstacle, new pathways will open. We'll discover that it's possible to develop tools to address human problems appropriately and effectively.

Once we harnessed the forces of gravity, we not only learned not to sit under apple trees, we learned how to fly to the moon. Let's call that force "Human Nature." From now on, when I refer to Human Nature, try to think of it as a thing. Like gravity, it's a very complex thing that often causes problems. But it's not a good thing or a bad thing; it's just a thing.

"Accepting our own nature" doesn't mean that anything goes! Bad things can happen as a result of human dynamics; I'm very aware of that. I'm suggesting that we have a better chance of mastering those forces if we approach conflicts from a different vantage point. Instantly labeling people as bad, stupid or crazy is divisive. We go back and forth until a tipping point is reached and an all-out war begins.

Much potential beauty lies in the atmosphere between people, between our instinct to fight and our instinct to flee. We need to create safe, open spaces where people who are different can breathe together.

3

Where We Are on the Evolutionary Continuum: Intellectually Brilliant; Emotionally...Not So Much

Research demonstrates that our core beliefs are hard-wired. They can't easily be changed, if they can be changed at all, with data and arguments.

Our cognitive template—the framework within which we perceive and interpret the world—represents a precipitant of genetics and epigenetics, early experiences and the way we learned to interpret reality. For example (statistically only; this is *not* true of every individual), it's been shown that liberals tend to be more flexible, adaptive and creative while conservatives tend to be more structured, loyal and watchful. Each has different perspectives on parenting and their MRIs are different. Neither is good or bad; they're just different.

All of us have unique identities and worldviews. We need them. Large groups need them too. Our identity is our psychological skin. It's the container that holds us together and protects us against threatening outside stimuli. Boundaries are necessary to preserve bodily integrity and to survive. If we took in every new idea and made it our own, "we" would no longer exist.

Dr. Vamik Volkan, the psychoanalyst who mediates between large groups to help prevent war, points out that large groups have identities analogous to individual identities. Countries, religions, and racial and ethnic groups share a complex history, culture, symbols, traumas and glories. In times of peace our individual identities are most important, but when our "tents" are shaken, our group identities rise to the surface and we speak as with one voice.

What's the identity that matters most to you? Someone who feels like an integral part of the black community might feel uncomfortable at a table with a white police officer. A person who grew up Palestinian might not be comfortable interacting with an Israeli. It might feel weird to collaborate on a group project with classmates wearing hijabs and yarmulkes if you're an atheist wearing a tank top and tattoos. A co-worker who campaigns for the candidate you can't stand might be hard to sit with at lunch. In individual situations you could probably make it work, but if there's a massive societal problem impacting one of those large groups, relationships might become intolerable and lead to overt fighting.

Picture yourself in those settings, or in a similar, more personal one. Can you feel the *I'm okay; they're okay* dynamic coexisting with *It feels uncomfortable to be with these people and I wish I didn't have to?* That's human nature. That discomfort represents a force that simply exists. Don't think of it as good or bad. It's normal to feel uncomfortable in the presence of someone who comes from a different cultural or ideological center. Don't blame yourself if you feel that way, and don't blame others if they do. ***Start with***

the premise that it's human nature to think and feel one of those ways, or both ways at the same time.

Identities may be essential for our physical and psychological survival, but they present a serious problem for the growth of our species. If you give people who see the world from one perspective data that seems contradictory to their beliefs, it takes less than a second for most of us to reframe that information in a way that fits our existing point of view. It's called "cognitive bias." Because of the way we evolved, our species can't easily assimilate a foreign body, physically or psychologically. The "backfire effect" suggests that when we're presented with contradictory evidence, our beliefs get stronger.

We're capable of some measure of empathy toward people with whom we're predisposed to empathize—a good mother or teacher might intuit what the children need and a good actor might "become" a character for the duration of a film—but in general, we're not capable of inhabiting the psychic reality of people who are very different from ourselves. As a result, we tend to experience difference as threatening.

Bad things happen, therefore there's no God.
Bad things happen because God gave us free will.

Poor people can't succeed because societal forces prevent it.
Poor people can't succeed because they lack the motivation.

If you agree with one of the above statements, it's probably hard to imagine having a conversation with someone who believes the opposite. How would you begin, other than with a useless argument or an insult?

Our species evolved in this way for a reason.

According to Dr. Volkan, as our brains developed, we moved from fighting for food and sex to fighting for more abstract concepts like power, prestige, honor, glory and identity. The implication is that as Homo sapiens grew psychologically, we developed complex individual and group identities that made us separate and distinct from one another. We now suffer from a tragic flaw in our genetic and psychological program; a flaw that prevents us from the kind of empathy that would be needed to solve problems of human difference.

"Sapiens" means "wise." We've become too hardened in our differences and too focused on external "hard data" in the search for understanding and insight. ***With no methodology for bridging these powerful human divides, our species is rapidly losing its capacity for wisdom.***

We can't keep blaming ourselves for being human. But if blaming doesn't work, we're still stuck. If we need our different identities and our species isn't built to empathize deeply or communicate effectively across complex human barriers, how can we hope to resolve conflicts? If we keep going this way, we won't ever figure out if there is a God or how to deal with the problem of poverty. We can elect a new leader or enforce a new law if our side wins 51% of the vote, but we can't work collectively. We can't address distortions, shift paradigms, and discover new and overarching truths the way we can in fields where hypotheses can be tested and facts verified. Scientific models will shift as new information arises—Isaac Newton's model gave way to relativity and quantum mechanics—but our gods and our politics are likely to survive until we kill each other in their name.

Humankind's intellectual achievements far surpass what we've achieved in the social/emotional arenas. At this point in human history, we're not able to move forward in the evolution of the dynamic constellation that distinguishes humans from other species —our humanity, our wisdom, and our ability to be conscious of ourselves.

A new evolutionary leap is necessary.

Without that evolutionary leap, we will continue to use our vast intellectual knowledge in clumsy, childlike, aggressive and destructive ways, perhaps leading to the premature death of our species.

We CAN make that leap. All we have to do is imagine it.

4

Imagining It: The Emergence of a New Language Leading to a Leap in Evolution

In the last chapter I said that we *can't* change our hard-wired brain pathways. In this chapter I'm going to walk that back. Research demonstrates that our brains *are* capable of neuroplastic changes. With a lot of hard work, we *can* change our brain pathways and pass those changes on to our children via education and epigenetics. But this can only happen incrementally. These transformations require insight, education, determination, skills and practice. They require much effort over long periods of time, individually and collectively.

The solution to the problem of intergroup conflict lies in the transitional space between two seemingly paradoxical ideas. On the one hand, we need to radically accept the fact that we can't change ourselves or one another. We have to stop blaming ourselves for being who we are. On the other hand, if we look in a different direction and work hard to make change happen, we will discover that *our species is capable of changing not just how we think, but also the brain pathways that lie beneath our usual and customary ways of thinking.*

The change I'm envisioning won't happen because people across a divide yell at us that we're stupid and we have to think differently. It will happen when we realize the need for *all of us* to learn to think differently...to imagine what that learning would involve...and to invest in the hard work necessary to accomplish it.

It's not that other guy who needs to change. It's our species.

Earlier stages of evolution emerged organically. Our ancestors didn't decide to make those changes happen; they just happened. But at this moment in the history of our species, the body part that's most fragile and most in need of transformation is our consciousness. I sincerely and powerfully believe that we're capable of changing our consciousness, consciously.

The next leap in the evolution of our species will be in our brains and our minds. It will be made with conscious understanding and conscious intent, as a new language emerges for communication across human divides.

What do I mean by "language"? Music has a language. You can read that language if you studied it, not if you didn't. Immersion in that language enables people with an intuitive sense of rhythm, emotionality, physical dexterity, passion and determination to make the leap to the Philharmonic. Computer science has a language, enabling talented experts in the field to work together to develop humankind's ability to communicate across massive physical divides. Physics has a language. Mastering it allows scientists and engineers to work together to send spaceships to other planets. Other fields have languages too; languages that appear foreign to those not immersed in the work. Try reading a medical journal, an economics article or a philosophy book and you'll see what I mean.

The complex language underlying emotional discourse can be experienced in Plato, Shakespeare, Freud, theology, history, political science, cognitive science, education and many other fields. Each has a theory and methodology that is codified and taught, but they're separate and distinct from each another. As we immerse ourselves in those fields, the languages we use become separate and distinct. We lose our ability to talk across disciplines.

Human understanding needs a language all its own, an Emotional Literacy that synthesizes insights from multiple disciplines. It must be codified and taught, using theory, literature, thought experiments and daily exercises, until it exists on a par with other major subjects in a K-12-PhD curriculum. Emotional Literacy needs to be taught and practiced until our species becomes fluent, until the best are recognized and supported in their rise to leadership.

Once we can develop that language, write it down and immerse ourselves in learning it, new brain pathways will slowly open and be passed on to future generations. The language of human discourse will become more intuitive, and human psychology and communication will enter a new evolutionary phase.

When I get on a plane, I trust that the people who designed, built and are flying that plane spent many years studying rocket science. In contrast, when I hear world leaders talk about where and when to send rockets to kill people in faraway lands, I hear children, sometimes, bullies, in a playground. *My worldview is superior to yours; I don't understand you; you scare me and therefore you have to die.*

If we don't change the paradigm soon, our species *will* die. Forget mastering climate change. The emotional climate may blow us back to the Stone Age first.

Mother nature exists within us as well as outside of us. Both climates are what they are, but both are shifting and becoming toxic. Revolutions in technology are bringing us too close together to allow us to live comfortably with separate and distinct belief systems. The physical climate and the emotional climate both present real and present dangers to the continued growth of our species. It's another inconvenient truth that we need to address the latter problem as well as the former…and we need to do it fast.

How? Analogies can be made to the top-down, bottom-up approach to climate change. If my model is going to take root, global initiatives and government regulations are needed. At the same time, individuals must work—separately and together—toward the psychological equivalent of "going green." Happily-ever-after is not the goal of either initiative. We live in a universe with a life span and we can't abort change except to a small degree. But we can anticipate and adapt better than we presently do. We *are* capable of working together to harness the forces of nature, including our own nature, in new ways.

Al Gore's documentary *An Inconvenient Truth* was released in 2006. Before that time, scientists worked hard to compile the necessary data, but Gore's film was the tipping point that brought the problem to the consciousness of the general public. Green careers and climate change agreements are now a thing.

I want this book to serve the same purpose as that film. The data we need are all available, in multiple separate disciplines. I want to pull these data together and present then from a different vantage point, in a way that will lead to a collective *aha* moment.

Our body parts are symmetrical, but one side dominates and leads. That happens in the human arena too, but only when one side wins a narrow margin over the other and becomes the "dominant party" or the "dominant faith." In the political arena, large groups move clumsily between left and right without an overarching vision or a shared horizon. In the religious arena we wear blinders to other perspectives on the problem of God, again with no overarching vision or shared horizon.

In today's world, the human experience is coming into conflict with science and technology. Our moral compass is transitioning from religion and ethics to hacking and tracking. *You'd better not misbehave, because someone will post a photo on Facebook!* Soon, genetic testing will allow us to choose the fetus we prefer to give birth to and imagine the disease from which we're likely to die. If we're in emotional pain, there's a pill for that. If we're psychotic, the pill will be tracked so an outside force will know if we've taken it.

The human experience must return to leading, not following, science and technology. If it does not, humans will become robots, robots will become human and our species will die from a cancer in our most valued body part: a part that I'll call, for want of a better word, our "soul."

This seismic change will not happen because we want it to or because evolution will magically intervene. It will happen when we realize the need for it; imagine what that "it" is or could be; and work together to coax it into existence.

A new academic track must be designed and piloted for children of all ages, until Emotional Literacy emerges as a new language for communicating across human divides. After much teacher education, that language must be given the same weight in the curriculum as the other major subjects and integrated with them.

Section II
The Language

5

Discovering the Language by Trying to Speak It

How does society give birth to a language that doesn't exist yet? First you have to imagine it. The best way to imagine a language isn't by reading a book about it, but by setting the stage for it to emerge and then trying to speak it. I haven't written the Human Understanding and Emotional Literacy vocabulary and grammar book yet, but I can tell you how you can visit that place and make a clumsy first effort.

Humanize the people you may think of as crazy, ignorant, against you, or with whom you have nothing in common. Talk to them, stay in the room when disturbances arise and figure out how to make it work.

Remember, prejudice (I prefer "pre-judgment" because it has fewer negative connotations) isn't just about race, gender and class; it's about intellect and thinking styles. Let go of your instinct to criticize and judge; instead, try to have a conversation with someone whose point of view or way of communicating doesn't make sense to you. I don't mean ISIS; that's for the PhD program. I mean the people in your life who behave in ways that you don't understand, don't like, or experience as wrong, offensive or ignorant.

If you're on social media, invite the people you blocked and unfriended back into the arena. Maybe you stopped responding to them because of extreme political differences. Maybe you're on the Israeli side and they support the Palestinians, or maybe one of you interprets everything as the will of God and the other is fed up with that. Maybe mental disorders are involved, or just differences in the way you see the world and communicate what you see. Maybe one of you speaks from gut feeling and the other requires documentation. Maybe one of you is more emotional and the other more intellectual. Maybe one has a graduate degree and the other barely finished high school. Maybe one of you is comfortable with fake news and the other is horrified by it. Maybe morality is important to one of you and the other is okay getting away with things. Maybe they attack you when you talk about something you're passionate about. Maybe you do the same to them.

Think of these differences the way you might think about differences in race, gender, sexuality and class structure. Is there a difference between thinking "S/he's an idiot" and thinking "S/he's a nigger"? Isn't one just as hurtful and distancing as the other? We're used to the language of "stupid" and "crazy" the way we once were used to the n-word and the f-word. That needs to change if we have any hope of communicating across thought process divides.

If our children or our students were calling each other morons and refusing to be their friends, we would try our best to put a stop to it, or at least try to understand what the problem is. Adults need to stop behaving like that too. It's hard because it's in our nature to be put off by difference; we try to protect ourselves from it. So we need to make a massive, collective effort to struggle against our own nature.

Note that I'm not saying this from a moral, ethical, religious or political center. I'm saying it because that way of thinking interferes with the emergence of a new language for communication across psychological divides.

Now that I told you to try it, I'll tell you that it will be difficult, maybe impossible to do it by yourself. You will need to engage with a partner or several people. Ideally, you will reference this book and announce that you're going to make the effort. If you don't, others will experience you as behaving in an idiosyncratic way. They won't see that there's an undiscovered language in the spaces between you, so the pull back to baseline will be massive and very hard to resist.

When a tipping point is reached and a large subgroup of people realize that their behavior—while human and understandable—doesn't work, shifts will begin to happen on a larger scale. Peer pressure will move the process forward and eventually the effort to communicate across human divides will move from idiosyncratic to expected.

If social media doesn't work for you, try it in person. Instead of trivia night or sports night or beer-in-a-bar night, invite your friends for a discussion about politics, religion, or some other issue that matters to you. It could be a conflict in your field. Personally, I would love to invite the classical psychoanalysts and the relational ones, or the pro-diagnosis-and-medication people and the anti-diagnosis-and-medication people to share a meal together.

Tell your friends that the "game" is to discover the grammar and syntax of a language that will help you talk across those divides and stay friends. Make it fun. Share what works and reflect on what doesn't. #talkacrossdivides #whatworks #doesntwork

If we can do this, our generation will go down in history as having catalyzed an evolutionary leap: consciously, deliberately and creatively. How cool is that?!

We need the "new game" part and the "How cool is that?!" part to motivate us. It's a daunting task, but the result could be very exciting.

6

Binocular Vision, Thinking Differences and Shared Playgrounds

If you do the exercise, you'll discover that it doesn't work to argue the topic. Something else has to happen first. The adversarial matrix between you needs to be softened. Don't attack the problem head on. Go off to the side.

One way is to ask the other person how they came to believe what they believe. *My father did that and I came out just fine*, or *My father did that and he was a jerk* are typical responses. Even if your instinct is to say, *So what?* or *No you didn't come out just fine!*—don't go there. Be curious, invite the person to talk about his/her childhood and share your own similar-but-different experiences. Remember that your beliefs come from a personal center too and are probably equally distorted as a result. Be curious about your own distortions and try not to be too triggered by theirs.

Another dynamic likely to arise is thought process differences. For example, some people are more dramatic and creative and less invested in hard data. I'm like that. I think in simple lines, broad strokes, narrative and imagination. My memory for facts isn't great. If I say that the sky is blue, and someone tries to discuss it using scientific research on color theory, the rods and cones in our eyes, the problem of color blindness and the philosophy of color, I'm going to want to turn that person off. *The sky is f'ing blue, except when it's pink at sunset!*

At the same time, I'm aware that those who can reference clinical facts and controlled studies about color theory, color blindness and the nature of the atmosphere are necessary if we're going to share an overarching perspective. I'll try hard to look at it from other vantage points and learn what I need to learn to help expand our collective knowledge about the appearance of the sky and what it implies. ***Art needs science and science needs art.***

A similar dynamic arises in my work. I tend to look at my psychiatric patients as complex individuals with complex narratives, powerful passions, conflicts and defenses. At the same time, I'm expected to document a checklist of symptoms and a diagnosable disorder for which there is a numerical code, a cost-effective treatment and the perfect drug. I find merging those two vantage points to be difficult and jarring. At the same time, I'm aware that other people think differently than I do. They find the latter method to be very useful. Patients react differently too. Some embrace the medical model and others don't. Each perspective is one-sided, but each complements the other and is necessary. Sometimes one perspective is most effective, sometimes the desire for one over the other is defensive. Some people want to prescribe and use drugs because they're afraid of looking within themselves, while others might insist on talking because they're afraid of medication.

You'll see my thinking style throughout this book. When I use concepts like "brain pathways" and "neuroplasticity," I'm using them in a way that bridges the divide between hard science and metaphor. I'm saying that our brains are wired in a particular way so we can't be mad at each other for our unique patterns of thinking, but I'm not referencing specific scientific data because I'm not that familiar with cutting edge research (which will have changed by the time you read this anyway). Attempts to accurately document and reference every concept would take me too far afield, invite distracting challenges and turn me off to my own work. I know this book will lack something as a result, but I hope it might be more readable to those who aren't scientifically inclined and will stimulate those who are to contribute to later discussions.

A metaphor that I like a lot is "binocular vision." If you're programmed to see the world from the perspective of a left eye, that landscape is all you'll be able to see and you'll assume that that's what reality looks like. But if you understand that there exists a right eye that sees the world from a different vantage point, you'll become interested in the way the other eye sees...or at least not be put off by it. Like two eyes focusing on a shared horizon, eventually you'll adapt to each other and move forward with clarity, perspective and the perception of depth. It's still likely that one side will need to be dominant and leading at any particular time, but the body politic with have a much better chance of bridging the "corpus callosum" and moving forward together. Liberals and conservatives can do that; so can religious people and atheists. Creative and data-driven people can work well together, too. I hope some scientists are intrigued enough to help me document my ideas, challenge me and help me take my work in new directions. I need those researchers and people with data. I need to focus, with them, on a shared horizon.

This may sound good, but in the real world these differences can be very triggering. One person will paint a picture of how important individual freedom is, and another will immediately counter with, *But what about all those guns?!* One person will say, *The climate is changing and we're responsible,* and the other will respond with, *You environmentalists are always trying to distract from the need to....* When such conflicts arise, look away from the content and think about the way you're communicating. Be curious. What's most important to you and to the other person? Why does that dynamic matter so much to them? To you? How do you express yourselves? What's on the surface and what lies beneath? *How did you become interested in the environment?* might be a bridging discussion. Freedom is a fascinating topic. Go there and lay down your gun control arguments until you deepen a philosophical discussion of individual and collective freedom as well as the personal experiences that led to your choice of political position.

A fundamental rule would be this: if you're triggered by a potentially adversarial conflict with a difficult person, go off to the side until you find an arena where you can play together.

7

More Complex
Thought Process Differences

Have you heard people talk about defense mechanisms? They're real, at least until we come up with a better model. We all use them to avoid thinking about painful events and feeling the emotions associated with them. Defense mechanisms usually develop early in life and exist outside of conscious awareness, but sometimes they're deliberate. When they're pointed out slowly, with empathy and respect, we can often begin to see them.

Here are a few examples. See if you can begin to recognize them in yourself and in other people. When you do, think about ways to gently and appropriately challenge them.

Repression is when you bury a memory because it's too painful to think about. Over time it fades completely. *Yeah, my parents got divorced. I'm not sure, but I think it was sometime in elementary school.* If you're talking to a person who doesn't remember something, consider the possibility that the memory would be more painful to dredge up than they realize. You might get them thinking if you respond with, *Gee, I vividly remember the day my parents told me about their divorce. I was so upset and mad. Was it no big deal for you, or did you try hard not to think about it?*

Suppression is more deliberate: you're not going to think about that. *Yeah, my parents are getting divorced. Want to go shopping?* You might respond with, *Sure. Maybe you'll want to tell me more about it over lunch.*

Denial is when you don't accept an aspect of reality. Substance abusers tend to use denial because it helps them look away from the severity of their problem. *I like to drink, but I'm not an alcoholic.* People often take offense when you directly confront them with their denial. Sometimes it's okay to let it go, but if the problem that arises from it is severe and destructive—*Yeah, my stomach hurts all the time lately, but I'm sure it's just because I love spicy food*—it needs to be confronted, often repetitively by more than one person.

Projection is a tough one. That's when you attribute to others feelings and thoughts that you need to ward off in yourself. *You think I'm stupid! Everyone thinks I'm gay! My co-workers are so incompetent that I can't do what I need to do! My family resents me and they're conspiring to undermine me!* The defense is unconscious, so the person genuinely believes it; often there's a kernel of truth that makes it particularly hard to confront. Paranoid psychosis uses projection in ways that are vastly out of touch with reality. *The CIA planted a device in the wall so they can spy on me.* Paranoia is very hard to deal with. Maybe when your grandchildren take the PhD program they can figure out new methods.

Rationalization is when you use seemingly rational reasons to justify behavior. *Yeah, I cut class again today. There was nothing going on and the teacher doesn't care. I'll ace that class anyway.* How might you respond if your friend said that?

Splitting is when you divide people into all good and all bad with no nuance. *Democrats care about people; Republicans are racist and selfish.* Splitting often coexists with **idealization** and **devaluation**. Your friend's new boyfriend was perfect and wonderful until he asked her to split the bill for dinner. *What a selfish creep he turned out to be!* If your friend said that to you, you might point out that it may or may not be about pure selfishness. He may be tight on money or he may believe that men shouldn't be responsible for paying all the bills, especially if the woman also has a good job. Invite your friend to think about nuance, but accept that it may be hard for her to do.

Displacement is when a feeling or thought is moved from a threatening place to a more benign place. It might be said that O.J. Simpson displaced his rage and aggression onto the football field. As you can see from that example, sometimes displacement can be helpful and other times it's a problem. When the defense no longer works effectively, powerful feelings can be unleashed.

Reaction formation happens when you convince yourself that you feel the opposite of the way you actually do feel. *I love my boyfriend's pit bulls. They're sweet.*

Dissociation often happens as a result of trauma. Severe forms used to be called "multiple personality disorder," but milder forms are common. People "step away from themselves" in different ways, often with a sense that they or the setting they're in is unreal. A woman being raped might stare at the ceiling and hypnotize herself as a way of escaping from the experience. Later, when she feels threatened, that same experience of separating herself from reality will happen outside of conscious awareness.

Intellectualization happens when a person represses an emotion associated with a thought. Your friend was diagnosed with a life-threatening illness, but instead of being scared, she does all the research and explains in great detail the medical aspects of her treatment and the credentials of her doctors. Depending on the situation, you might let her keep her defenses and listen carefully to her presentation, or you might gently invite her to share what she's feeling as well as what she's thinking.

Isolation of affect is when she says, *Yeah, I have cancer, but it's okay. I got this.* Isolating the idea of cancer from other frightening associations preserves emotional equilibrium.

Undoing is when you behave in an opposite way from the way that you feel, e.g. when you find yourself being overly nice to someone after having thoughts about hating them.

Defense mechanisms can be, and often are, healthy. **Sublimation** and **altruism** allow us to redirect forbidden impulses into socially appropriate arenas. **Humor** is an excellent way to deal with pain, unless it transitions to ridicule and hurtful sarcasm.

What can you do with this list? Think about defense mechanisms as ubiquitous. They're human ways of harnessing painful thoughts and feelings; all of us use them. You haven't yet taken my still-imaginary Emotional Literacy curriculum, so don't expect yourself to instantly recognize them, but do stop yourself from rolling your eyes when you see someone who you think is "in denial," "rationalizing" or "projecting." Humanize them and respond with empathy, perhaps with gentle confrontation if it seems appropriate and helpful.

When you see a dynamic that triggers you to respond with criticism, think about whether there's a different, more empathic way to look at the problem. If your instinct is to say, *Congressional representatives are all corrupt!* you might reframe it as, *Congressional representatives have to preserve an attitude of confidence while they figure out how to be true to themselves, true to their constituents, work with people from the other side and get reelected. That must be hard, maybe impossible. I wonder if I could do that....*

The list below is more complicated: Formal Thought Disorders from the Johns Hopkins Psychiatry Guide. It's a standard that psychiatrists use when they diagnose people with major mental illnesses.

Don't feel that you need to understand these descriptors in detail. I'm sharing it to show you how complex the human mind is and how learning about it is important for all of us. As long as these tools remain in the hands of mental health professionals, it preserves a power dynamic and an illness dynamic that doesn't have to be there. When mental health professionals use these categories, it's so we can label you as "sick" or "disordered." Meanwhile, all of us can and should see ourselves in these lists, in more subtle forms.

Formal thought disorder descriptors (adapted from the Thought, Language, and Communication scale).[2]

- Poverty of speech: restricted quantity of speech. Brief, unelaborated responses
- Poverty of content of speech: adequate speech quantity with prominent vagueness and inappropriate level of abstraction
- Pressure of speech: increased rate and quantity of speech. Speech may be loud and difficult to interrupt
- Distractible speech: topic maintenance difficulties due to distraction by nearby stimulus
- Tangentiality: replies to questions are off-point or totally irrelevant
- Derailment (loosening of associations): spontaneous speech with marked impairments in topic maintenance
- Incoherence (word salad, schizophasia): severe lack of speech cohesion at the basic level of syntax and/or semantics within sentences

---

2 See www.hopkinsguides.com/hopkins/view/Johns_Hopkins_Psychiatry_Guide/787025/all/Thought_Disorder Last updated: August 2, 2017.

- Illogicality: marked errors in inferential logic
- Clanging: speech in which word choice is governed by word sound rather than meaning. Word choice may show rhyming or punning associations
- Neologism: the creation of new "words"
- Word approximations: unconventional and idiosyncratic word use
- Circumstantiality: excessively indirect speech. Speech is liable to be over-inclusive and include irrelevant detail
- Loss of goal: difficulty in topic maintenance in reference to failure to arrive at the implicit goal of a statement
- Perseveration: excessive repetition of words, ideas, or subjects
- Echolalia: speech repeats words or phrases of interviewer
- Blocking: interruption of speech while ostensibly in pursuit of a goal
- Stilted speech: odd language use that may be excessively formal, pompous, outdated or quaint
- Self-reference: the patient is liable to refer the subject of conversation back to him/herself
- Paraphasic error (phonemic): word mispronunciation, slip of the tongue
- Paraphasic error (semantic): substitution of an inappropriate word to make a specific statement

Are you the silent type? Can't stop talking/posting? Do you lose your train of thought? Do you belabor a point? Is it sometimes hard to find words to express yourself? Do you take ideas out of context and hyper-focus on details or the part that matters most to you? Do you reference lots of facts or do you respond from a personal, emotional center? Do you make problems into jokes or invent new words? Do you think more abstractly or more concretely? When asked to read something, do you respond emotionally to the content or is your instinct to edit the grammar and syntax? Do you repeat yourself? Do people find you hard to follow? Far ends of these continua can be obsessive-compulsive, attention deficit, manic, depressed, psychotic or personality-disordered, but they can also be artists, lawyers, accountants, comedians or members of the clergy. People on the autistic spectrum often present with idiosyncratic speech.

We can take these lists, normalize them by rewording them in a way that's less extreme, use them as examples of different thinking styles, and learn how to respond to these differences appropriately and effectively.

I'm sure you don't think of your instinctual responses as "diagnosing," but in a sense that's something we all do. My field's "personality disorder" is your "asshole!" Honor your very human instinct to think those thoughts, then let go of them and try to figure out a way to bridge the divide between you and the other person. Remember, people who come from a different psychological center are disturbing, but as we come to understand them better, they'll be less so.

8

Talking to Psychosis

In 2011, Jared Lee Loughner killed six people and wounded 13, including U.S. Representative Gabrielle Giffords, his target. He was floridly psychotic.

In a town meeting several years earlier, Loughner asked Rep. Giffords, "What is government if words have no meaning?" The question seemed meaningless and disturbing (ref: "formal thought disorders" in the previous chapter), so Giffords' people ushered him out of the room. He stalked her until he was able to shoot her.

Crazy guy, crazy question. Crazy people need to go away, right?

Try thinking about it this way: Loughner is a human being and he asked a question that meant something to him. Yes, it was oddly expressed, but what if Representative Giffords and the people who worked with her had taken that question, and him, seriously? He probably sounded like a "psycho," but what if they had understood that psychotic people lose their ability to think clearly in words? What if he was trying to say that words were losing their meaning for him and he was asking for the government's help with that problem? What if they had approached him with that level of empathy, tried to understand what he was asking and helped him get the mental health treatment he desperately needed?

A language to bridge human divides exists. All we have to do is uncover it. I suspect that people with a history of schizophrenia and other psychotic disorders could be of great help to us in that effort.

I'll never forget my first day in the psychiatric emergency room. When you begin to examine patients, you're given a script called a Mental Status Exam. You ask what the chief complaint is and you ask about the history of that problem, along with past and family history. Then you ask questions designed to address their thinking style. For example, "What brings you here?" could be responded to with, "The subway," "The voices," "I'm f'ing miserable," "My wife is a bitch," or "My hysterical mother thinks I'm gonna kill myself." "What's alike between an apple and an orange?" might elicit, "They're both fruit," "They're both round," "They're not alike, one is red and the other is orange," or "They're not alike, I like apples and I hate oranges."

You might also give the person a proverb. In this situation I asked the man, "What does it mean when they say people who live in glass houses shouldn't throw stones?" His instant reply was, "It means you shouldn't masturbate in public." I thought that was fascinating.

The man was diagnosed psychotic, but if you didn't know that, you might think it was the response of a comedian, or an image in a dream representing conflicts about sexuality and sexual expression. In a strange way, it was accurate.

A movement exists to remove or change the word "schizo-phrenia" because it's stigmatizing and not very helpful. It's been compared to the word "fever" as a symptom, not a specific disease entity. I'm ambivalent because diagnoses are tied with medication choices that need to hit a particular target if they're going to be effective, but as long as we can see through both eyes at the same time with a shared horizon in focus, we can go a long way toward helping struggling people AND allowing them to help society through improved ability to communicate their experience.

People with unusual thinking styles can help us uncover and codify the language that we're going to coax into existence. Let's not push these people away. Let's not try too hard to medically repair the damage to their brains and assume that's all that's neces-sary. Brains, minds and spirits can't easily be separated.

If we try, we'll discover that we can talk to, and learn much from, worthy human beings who experience the psychological phenomenon presently known as psychosis.

9

Individual vs.
Group Dynamics

I referenced Dr. Volkan earlier; I like his model a lot. According to him, individual people live under large group "tents." These tents are covered with memories and symbols of their people's past traumas and glories. A group's history is passed down through generations. In times of peace we don't pay much attention to our large group; we go about our lives as unique individuals. But when our large group is threatened, our group identity rises to the surface and we respond as a collective.

How does this problem come alive in everyday discourse? Someone will say, *Muslims/Jews/Christians are.... Black/White people are.... Rich/Poor people are.... Gay/Straight people are.... Polish/Chinese/Mexican people are....* Someone else will immediately respond with, *That's not true! I'm a member of that group and I'm not like that! You're prejudiced and stereotyping!* The discussion ends with embarrassment, frustration, hurt feelings and a dead end. That happens constantly, doesn't it?

A complex problem can be solved with a simple, obvious insight. *We are not our large group, but we come from that group and our group's history is part of who we are.* Separate the history and dynamics of your large group from your personal history and dynamics, but recognize that relationship and honor it. Realize that people from other groups are looking at your group's "personality" from a distance. Under certain circumstances, it's not wrong to look at a group from that perspective and comment on what you're seeing.

For example, to say that the history of black people in America is a history of trauma and abuse doesn't mean that your African-American neighbors felt abused as individuals or that they're entitled to be vengeful and retaliatory. But when a lot of black people get killed, a "tent" dynamic will rise to the surface and you may find your neighbors wearing Black Lives Matter t-shirts and being angry and defensive in a way that may appear exaggerated to you. Police officers—another large group collective—may become equally defensive in response. These responses aren't "bad," they're human and appropriate.

How do we deal with this aspect of our humanity? *Consider when you're speaking from a personal center and when you're speaking as a member of a collective. Listen for the same elements in others. Differentiate individual from group dynamics when you listen and when you speak, and don't blur the distinctions between them.* If you're responding as a representative of your large group, try introducing your response with, "Speaking as a member of x community, given the experiences of my people, when that kind of thing happens it makes me feel and think about...."

10
Playing with God

Okay, so you're starting to think about your annoying friends from a different vantage point. They're just being who they are, and so are you. You're going to try to tolerate their style of communicating, listen attentively to what they think, feel and believe, and consider whether they're coming from a personal center or if their personal communication also represents a large group dynamic.

But what if they're thinking something that makes no sense to you at all? If you're an atheist and your friend is immersed in the practice of his/her faith, what can you possibly say beyond, "I don't get it and I think you're wrong"? If one person thinks a newly-fertilized embryo is a human being and the other thinks it's a collection of cells, how can that conflict possibly be resolved by talking?

Don't talk about charged topics directly. Humanize each other and be interested in your differences. Find a new playground.

Free associate in different directions until you begin to enjoy the experience. It's typical for us to present ideas not as hypotheses to play with, but as What We Believe to Be True, Period. We present our ideas in ways that other people can only accept, challenge or ignore.

Consider that there's no such thing as a "wrong" idea, in the sense that it comes from somewhere and it means something. Psychoanalysts call it "psychic reality." An idea may not mean what you think it means, but it means something that can't and shouldn't be dismissed. It's not the same as moral equivalence or Truth-with-a-capital T, but it is a kind of truth. If something is experienced as real to one person, it's important to try to see the world from that vantage point. It won't be possible to "get it" at the same level of meaning and meaningfulness, but when you try, a little at a time over a long period of time, you'll begin to see the problem with that wider, two-eyed lens.

If you and the other person can do that, a bridge between you may arise that will turn out to be different from what either of you believe. Keep an open mind. Consider that religious people and non-religious people, or liberals and conservatives, are blind men examining an elephant and assuming that the part that they see is how the elephant really appears. Consider that there may be an elephant with an entirely different shape that hasn't come into focus yet. Consider the possibility that each of you sees one element more clearly than another. Imagine that the elephant is there to be found if you share your perceptions with each other in the right way and continue a dialogue over time.

One bridge that's important to consider is that between the literal and the metaphorical. Whether or not you believe in a literal God, God is a very real thing in humankind's history and present reality. The statement, "Religion is wrong" is equally wrong, because God is psychic reality to a huge subgroup of people. There has to be some kind of rightness to it. Put aside the divisive question about the literalness of Your God vs. My God vs. No God. Play with the metaphors together.

Here are some examples from my own imagination. I hope you'll play with these ideas with me without focusing on whether or not they're accurate:

For me, God is a question; a fascinating, not-yet-answered question. *Who are we? Where did we come from? Why are we here? Where are we headed?*

I don't know if God exists, but I'm pretty sure that our species couldn't survive if we could no longer ask that question. If you're not religious, you might be wondering why science alone can't answer it. Why does the question need a human face?

When I play with that question, I think about the fact that children need the gleam in the eye of a loving parent, along with structure and discipline, in order to survive and thrive. They need to mean something to someone. It doesn't matter if they have food, clothing and shelter. Without love, they'll die psychologically and perhaps physically. I think humankind needs the same thing in order to move forward as a species. Whether or not God is real and whether s/he really looks like one of the entities we presently imagine, I think our species needs that question, and it needs to give that question a human face.

I fear that our species is losing a worthy and accurate concept of God. As a result, we're losing meaning, the motivation to care for one another, self-regulating rituals, a shared reason for being and the drive to transcend our animal instincts.

Maybe the answer will turn out to be that we're nothing from nowhere, or maybe it will be that we're programmed by a higher power. Maybe that higher power closely resembles one of the gods descended from Abraham, or maybe it will turn out to be different from what any of us imagine. The "elephant" is one that we haven't discovered yet, but we have the capacity to inch closer to that discovery if we talk to one another in a different kind of way. *How do we reach God?* is equivalent to *How do we fly to the moon?* Centuries ago we thought that the earth was flat, the sun revolved around the earth and the word "gravity" didn't exist. We fought against each new scientific finding, but when we put our heads together we were able to land on the moon. I believe that we can find God/"God" in the same way.

Here's an example of a way that disparate ideas can come together in an original hypothesis, one that puts aside the question of whether Jesus is or is not God. I have some theories about Jesus that I haven't heard anywhere before. I have no idea if they're valid; I got them from playing. I'm using them as an example of the way that Catholicism, Freudianism, parenting theory, politics, art vs. science and the Wizard of Oz can be combined to open up new ways of looking. Take your disparate disciplines and different beliefs, free associate together and mix it up.

I was raised Catholic. I grew up believing in the Father, Son and Holy Spirit and that mine was the one true faith. Then I got older and met friends who came from other belief systems. I saw how beautiful religion was, how similar-but-different they were and also the harm that could be done in the name of God. WTF is this religion thing?!

Later I discovered psychoanalysis. In psychoanalysis, the mechanism of change is "transference." If your analyst shows interest, understands you, questions you, challenges you and presents new ideas in new ways, you will develop powerful feelings toward that person who comes to represent other figures in your life, and you will discover what it means to love, to hate and to know. That passion becomes the fuel for, and the defense against, the work of insight and change. Neurobiology will reframe and rename that concept, but for the purpose of this chapter "transference" is a nice way of explaining a phenomenon that we see all around us. The reasons we feel close to some people and put off by others has much to do with this phenomenon.

One day it occurred to me that Jesus was doing something very simple and very Freudian. Jesus was intuitively using Freud's transference model in an effort to catalyze large-scale societal change.

Jesus admonished the Jewish/Roman people, telling them to stop counting their money and be loving and generous to the poor people and the lepers. I imagine that must have stimulated a lot of conflict. Doesn't it sound like the same conflict that goes on now between liberals and conservatives in politics? What does it mean to keep your hard-earned money and be generous to the needy at the same time?

My hypothesis is that what happened with Jesus is the same thing that happens when an analyst makes a similar kind of disturbing confrontation. We call it "transference resistance." The analyst points out something that's jarring for the patient, a different way of looking at him/herself. Because it's painful, difficult or new, it's experienced as threatening. A typical response is to become defensively emotional. Instead of reflecting on whether there's painful truth to what the analyst is saying, the analyst is experienced as either the smartest analyst in the world or the most incompetent. Arguing about the emotional experience acts as a defense against grappling with the content of the intervention.

Jesus' way of presenting himself, as half God and half man, is similar to the way a good analyst presents him/herself. On the one hand, it's necessary to keep a distance in a way that invites analysands to imagine the analyst as having the capacity to help them change at the core of their being. There's something God-like and magical about that position. But it's equally necessary to keep two feet planted firmly on the ground, fully aware that analysts are also flawed human beings using a methodology that they studied for a very long time.

My hypothesis is that Jesus' confrontation about the need to be more loving and generous divided the population into the group that idealized him and the group that wanted him to go away. This conflict persisted over generations as people continued to talk and write about him long after his death, creating their own narrative that took on a life of its own. He was killed, but "He" remains alive after more than 2000 years. Why? I think it's because his original challenge and the transference resistances emerging from it have yet to be resolved.

We can't lay him to rest because the problems he confronted us with also remain alive. How can we give appropriately to people who do not have as much as we have while preserving our boundaries and what is rightfully ours? (Segue to politics....)

The Wizard of Oz did a variation of the same thing. He presented himself as a transference figure, the Great and Powerful Oz, knowing full well that he was just a little old man behind a curtain. Because they believed in his magic, Dorothy and her seemingly brainless, heartless and cowardly friends mustered the strength to confront their conflicts and melt the Wicked Witch. Their magical "analyst" could then emerge as the flawed human being that he was and they could all return home better for the experience. That's exactly how psychoanalysis works.

Parenting works in a similar way. When we're young, parents are magical, God-like figures that children love, hate, learn from, struggle with, and develop in relation to. After teaching them the art of melting witches, parents go back to being little old men and women behind a curtain. The child accepts that reality and becomes a confident and independent person.

Here's another theory about Jesus that I got from playing. In the Jewish doctrine, you can't speak the name of God or paint his image; icons are not allowed in the temple. When Jesus came along, He gave the G-d of the Jews a face that could be painted, a name that could be spoken, and "the greatest story ever told." Maybe those who were turned on by him were the more creative people and the ones who weren't were the more intellectual. It could be argued that Western art emerged out of Christianity, while the Jewish people have the most Nobel Prizes. Maybe there was something about Jesus and his mythology that divided the world into right brains and left brains.

Again, I'm not presenting these hypotheses to prove that my theories are true. I'm demonstrating that other ways of looking exist, can be fun to play with and can eventually lead to greater, unseen truths.

Was Jesus God? I don't know and I don't care. Demanding an answer to that question aborts the playful exchange across disciplines, modalities and metaphors. We're unlikely to answer that question in our lifetimes, but with the right tools, future generations will inch ever closer. I'd love to hear my Jewish and Muslim friends, and friends of other faiths, play with the metaphors and the important figures of their religions in a similar way, share their associations and challenge mine.

My basic point is not to convince you of something specific, but to demonstrate that *it's possible for different disciplines to come together in totally new ways and play with ideas until new hypotheses arise and take hold. If we continue to separate our disciplines, we will continue to argue about the number of angels that can dance on the heads of our separate and distinct pins.*

11

A Simple, Week-Long Emotional Literacy Curriculum

Are you ready to move on to something more concrete, something with a lesson plan that can be implemented right here and right now?

A few years ago, I developed a pilot project for middle school students that I called Emotional Imprint™. The name of the program is based on the following idea: *When you hold up your hands, from a distance they all look alike. They may be somewhat different sizes and colors, but they're impossible to distinguish. As you get closer, you'll see that the fingers are built differently, to serve different purposes. Get even closer and you'll see that each individual fingerprint is entirely distinct. It's possible to identify someone with complete accuracy from fingerprints alone.*

I suggest that we also have unique emotional imprints. How we think, feel and behave represents a complex precipitant of factors that make our personalities unique and uniquely able to impact the world. Just as we have unique fingerprints and carbon footprints, we also have unique emotional imprints on the people in our lives and the society in which we live.

If our individual "fingers" and our large-group, left and right "hands" work well together, we can accomplish marvelous things.

My organization successfully piloted week-long and semester-long versions of an academic curriculum that I imagined, Melissa Brand, Psy.D. designed, and social worker Sasha Diamond-Lenow taught to middle school students at Street Squash, a New York City-based sports and academic afterschool program.

At the beginning of the course students are assigned and imagine themselves as adult personas that they keep for the duration of the class, e.g. a bus driver, an investment banker, a disabled veteran, a teacher, a doctor, a chef, a farmer, a fast-food worker, a CEO, an unemployed actor or a famous musician. They receive salaries and tax brackets, write checks to the IRS, and use the rest of their income to create a budget. In the longer curriculum they're also given ages, races, genders and family structures. They do the research to buy or rent property and decide how the rest of their income will be used. What will it require to buy a house, a car, a pet? What will it cost to send their children to college? Students learn what taxes are and how they're used. They think about who among them will receive government benefits and where that money comes from. They learn about healthcare and health insurance. They learn about our political system, decide which party their characters are likely to support and host debates on issues of the day.

What's unique about this curriculum is the way it integrates emotional learning and academic learning. Students' initial reaction is typical: the rich and famous ones celebrate and the people with lower salaries or government benefits are disappointed. They often ask to exchange their lives for "better" ones. Discussions around this simple, human reaction are invaluable.

They leave the class with greater empathy for parents who have to make important short and long-term financial decisions when the students ask for a new pair of sneakers or college tuitions. They leave with the desire to say hi to their bus drivers. They're aware of dynamics that may arise if they find themselves with roommates from different races, socio-economic groups or political positions. They leave with a greater understanding of the way government works and the experiences that might motivate a person to take one or another political position. They also get some good math problems—taxes, loans, mortgages, budgets—along with the motivation to solve them.

Classes like these can be designed for children just entering school. They can deepen in learning and practice, integrating information and exercises from multiple disciplines, for the duration of their academic careers.

Here's how I imagine a K-12 academic track that integrates empathic imagination, neurobiology, psychoanalytic theory and methodology, cognitive science and other academic subjects.

In elementary school, a lesson might be this: *A classmate comes up to you in the playground and says, "Your sand castle is crooked." Let's list as many reasons as we can think of for why he or she might say that and let's think about how you might respond in each situation.*

Students might wonder if he was mean because his father was mean to him. Maybe she's competitive with you. The teacher might explain that for some people, crooked things make them anxious. Maybe your sand castle *is* crooked and it's your friend's clumsy way of offering to help. Some people are very direct and will say what they're thinking without the ability to empathize with the impact that statement might have on you.

Now imagine the same question posed as a homework assignment or test question for an older child: *Someone walks into your playground and says, "Your sand castle is crooked." List six different reasons why a person might say that to you and six different responses based on your hypothesis. Choose one of them and create an in-person or email dialogue designed to test it. What clues might tell you whether your hypothesis is accurate? Try to remain true to yourself and build a bridge to that person. Remember to take your own feelings into account. How important is it to "you" (your character doesn't have to be exactly like you) to work alone, to play with this person, to get help, to win the sand castle competition? What if she looks like she's going to knock it down? Consider what we learned about different motivations, thinking styles and coping mechanisms. Your dialogue doesn't have to lead to a happy resolution. It just has to be deep, complex and authentic.*

Now imagine the same question, posed metaphorically, for university students: *given that we all have our "castles in the sky"—the conscious and unconscious structures that define us to ourselves—choose a political or religious ideology. Think of a time in history, or in the present day, when one leader's worldview was challenged by another with the message, "Your castle in the sky is distorted." Write a paper on the way that dynamic was or is being addressed in historical context. Consider how a greater capacity for self-other awareness in the context of large group processes, political dynamics and leadership, group history, identity, belief systems, ways of thinking and communicating, etc., might or might not have led to a different outcome."* Imagine how complex, nuanced and accurate responses would be if the students had studied human dynamics academically, and tested their understanding as deepening thought experiments, for the previous 12 years.

Note that because this program presents psychodynamic tools as thought experiments that are experience-near but not boundary violating (academics should not be "therapy lite") deeper insights into human nature are able to rise to the surface. Personal insight, anti-bullying, and an opportunity for the most gifted to rise to the surface would be side effects of such a program.

Future generations would be able to recognize and vote for leaders who demonstrate proficiency in combining emotional strength, personal insight and integrity, creative vision, empathic imagination, dynamic complexity, and the ability to communicate effectively.

Section III
The Problem
of War

12

Why War? An Ineffective Dialogue Between Two Great Minds

In 1932, Albert Einstein wrote a letter to Sigmund Freud. He asked, in light of Freud's recent discoveries about the human mind, why we have war. This is an excerpt from that correspondence, later published as the monograph, *Why War?*[3]

> **Einstein:** *Is there any way of delivering mankind from the menace of war? It is common knowledge that, with the advance of modern science, this issue has come to mean a matter of life and death for civilization as we know it; nevertheless, for all the zeal displayed, every attempt at its solution has ended in a lamentable breakdown.... Only one answer is possible.*

---

3 Freud, S. (1933). "Why War?" *The Standard Edition of the Complete Psychological Works of Sigmund Freud, Volume XXII (1932-1936): New Introductory Lectures on Psycho-Analysis and Other Works*, pp. 195-216.

Because man has within him a lust for hatred and destruction. In normal times this passion exists in a latent state, it emerges only in unusual circumstances; but it is a comparatively easy task to call it into play and raise it to the power of a collective psychosis. Here lies, perhaps, the crux of all the complex factors we are considering, an enigma that only the expert in the lore of human instincts can resolve.... Is it possible to control man's mental evolution so as to make him proof against the psychosis of hate and destructiveness? Here I am thinking by no means only of the so-called uncultured masses. Experience proves that it is rather the so-called "intelligentsia" that is most apt to yield to these disastrous collective suggestions, since the intellectual has no direct contact with life in the raw but encounters it in its easiest, synthetic form—upon the printed page.... It would be of the greatest service to us all were you to present the problem of world peace in the light of your most recent discoveries, for such a presentation well might blaze the trail for new and fruitful modes of action.

Freud: *I expected you to choose a problem lying on the borderland of the knowable.... I was dumbfounded by the thought of my (of our, I almost wrote) incompetence; for this struck me as being a matter of practical politics, the statesman's proper study.... [You have] taken the wind out of my sails!.... You surmise that man has in him an active instinct for hatred and destruction.... I entirely agree with you...this instinct functions in every living being, striving to work its ruin and reduce life to its primal state of inert matter. Indeed, it might well be called the "death instinct"; whereas the erotic instincts vouch for the struggle to live on.... The upshot of these observations, as bearing on the subject in hand, is that there is no likelihood of our being able to suppress humanity's aggressive tendencies... as you too have observed, complete suppression of man's aggressive tendencies is not in issue; what we may try is to* *divert it into a channel other than that of warfare.... The ideal conditions would obviously be found in a community where every man subordinated his instinctive life to the dictates of reason.... Why do we, you and I and many another, protest so vehemently against war, instead of just accepting it as another of life's odious importunities? The basis of our common hatred of war is this: we cannot do otherwise than hate it. Pacifists we are, since our organic nature wills us thus to be.... Now war runs most emphatically counter to the psychic disposition imposed on us by the growth of culture; we are therefore bound to resent war, to find it utterly intolerable. With pacifists like us it is not merely an intellectual and affective repulsion, but a constitutional intolerance, an idiosyncrasy in its most drastic form. And it would seem that the aesthetic ignominies of warfare play almost as large a part in this repugnance as war's atrocities.... With kindest regards and, should this expose prove a disappointment to you, my sincere regrets.*

These are excerpts that I chose, but I chose them for a reason. Can you see why these two great minds couldn't move forward toward solving the problem? **Freud missed something very important, and Einstein never called him on it.**

On the one hand, Freud appears to agree with Einstein when he states that, "every man has within him a lust for hatred and destruction." He even gives it a name, the "death instinct." But he goes on to say that the two of them are somehow above it. Other people have that "innate instinct," but he and Einstein have an "intellectual and affective repulsion...a constitutional intolerance."

Uh, no. Both can't be true at the same time, Sigmund—at least not without further exploration. If it's true that the propensity for war lies within us all, you might have gone much further if you had tried to discover that propensity within yourself like you did with the sexual instincts. It sounds like you didn't want to take up Einstein's challenge so you looked away from it. That's an example of what you would call a "defense mechanism," isn't it?

Freud also doesn't respond to Einstein's other challenge, that it's the "intelligentsia" that is *most* apt to "yield to these disastrous collective suggestions, since the intellectual has no direct contact with life in the raw but encounters it in its easiest, synthetic form: upon the printed page." He not only ignores Einstein's idea—a challenge to the academic/liberal left in the present day!—he reinforces the problem by implying that intellect is the solution. Freud envisions "a community where every man subordinated his instinctive life to the dictates of reason." Doesn't that sound like a world filled with "intelligentsia," which is the exact opposite of what Einstein is suggesting? Neither of them seems to have noticed that.

Did you also notice the way that Einstein and Freud blurred the distinctions between large groups that fight wars and individual people who harbor "aggressive tendencies"?

This is just my fantasy, but I imagine that Einstein's effort to reach out to him might have made Freud feel uncomfortable. Do you see how apologetic he is? Maybe the challenge by a mind he thought was greater than his own threw him off his game. Freud was usually a clear and confident thinker, but when people feel anxious they often don't respond as they normally would.

Whatever the reasons, Freud got defensive and Einstein didn't go further in challenging those defenses. Something interesting might have happened in that dialogue between two great minds, but nothing did.

13
Why War? A Theory and a Methodology

I will now attempt to join Einstein and Freud's conversation, and deepen it.

Is there any way of delivering mankind from the menace of war?

My answer is yes, there is a way of delivering humankind from the menace of war. But first we need to realize two things.

1) The source of that menace lies within us all, not just those other "bad guys." We will not be saved by intellectual arguments presented by so-called "intelligentsia" who claim to be pacifists and we will not be saved by physical efforts to keep "them" away or wipe "them" off the face of the earth. Only when we realize that the Problem of War lies within ourselves—each and every one of us—will we discover that our species possesses the power to do something about it.

2) ***We need to learn to fight "wars" in words.*** We will never make the leap from war to peace if we alternate mandates to love one another with threats of violence when that inevitably doesn't happen. ***We need to create transitional spaces for powerful feelings and fantasies to emerge, be given expression in words, and be tolerated and explored by the people against whom they're directed.*** This needs to happen slowly. It takes a long time to humanize a person or group of people who may seem primitive, inhuman or just-plain wrong, attempt to communicate with them, and have that communication be effective enough for powerful feelings to be tamed and replaced by mutual insight and pathways for solutions. As I said in earlier chapters, even psychotic people are capable of understanding and being understood, and they have much to teach us. If we don't try, people with one-sided or delusional thinking will act on their fantasies until we're all fighting imaginary demons with real weapons.

We live in an instant-gratification world. Slowing down might seem like going backwards, but the ability to tolerate ambiguity, paradox, dynamic conflict and the time it takes to resolve them would be evidence of profound forward movement. ***Humanity must return to leading, not following, science and technology. And humans change slowly.***

Allow me to demonstrate. Watch me start a war, right now.

Instead of saying the usual and customary, *Unfortunately, anti-Semitism remains a global problem and is very, very bad,* I'm going to reframe the problem in this way: *The continued presence of anti-Semitism means that a lot of people in the world still don't like Jews.*

You may be feeling punched in the stomach right now, and you may want to punch me back. How dare I suggest that?!

All I'm doing is stating a fact. I'm reframing the more tolerable first sentence in a different but equally accurate way. But the way I said it is so triggering that it hurts just to hear it. But if it can be posed that way, people who harbor negative feelings toward Jews will become more comfortable entering the discussion. They will be able to say, *Yeah, I don't like Jewish people because....*

Given that the history of the Jewish people is of thousands of years of hatred and genocide, that won't be easy to tolerate. It will be painful, offensive and re-traumatizing to listen to. But we're human beings, and human beings can't make their feelings go away because they're mandated to. If words aren't used, weapons will be.

Maybe a discussion will proceed as follows:

Person A: *I don't trust them because Jewish people are money-hungry.*

Person B: *Did you know that a lot of Jewish people entered the field of business because they were shut out of other fields?*

Person A: *Yeah, I get that, but they still think they like money and they feel chosen and entitled to run the world.*

Person C: *If there's any truth to what you're saying—and I'm not saying there is—maybe we can spin it differently. Maybe a lot of members of that "tent" are smart and driven to succeed, are left-brained and have business backgrounds, and they want to overcome their past and prove that they're not inferior. Is that so bad?*

Person A: *Well...I gotta think about that.... Still seems like there's something not right, but I'm not sure....*

Person D: *I'm curious about what it means to be "chosen" in different faiths. I'm Christian. I was taught that God chose me to go to heaven to be with him and I should teach others about Jesus so they could go to heaven too. Jewish people don't proselytize, do they? From* *an outside perspective it seems kinda selfish to keep all that chosen-ness to yourself. But proselytizing seems aggressive and selfish too, in a different kind of way. What do you think the difference is?*

I'm just free associating, but can you see what I'm doing? I'm taking a very charged idea, inviting people from different perspectives to talk about that idea and tolerate the discomfort of doing so, and I'm trying to soften the matrix between them and pose some new questions so it doesn't regress to an intolerable place.

Here's another idea that will be very triggering.

Person A: *Pedophilia is a sexual orientation that can't be changed.*

Person B: *How dare you say that! Everything that involves sex with children is wrong and must be unconditionally rejected!*

Can you see what happened? Person B was so triggered by the equation of pedophilia and normality that s/he made the leap to the assumption that Person A was suggesting that sex with children should be considered acceptable behavior. But that may not have been what Person A was saying. Person A might have been suggesting that if it's true that sexual desire for children begins early in life and can't be changed, society might consider finding ways to ally with potential pedophiles to try to help them emerge from the shadows and find solutions before child abuse and crimes are committed.

We could do similar thought experiments with the never-ending debate about whether poor people or rich people are the more selfish, demanding and entitled, or how to address the problem of wealth and poverty without encroaching on individual freedoms. Abortion is another problem that can be discussed once we figure out new ways to approach it. (Try adding the time dimension to the question, *What is life and when does it begin?*)

It's been demonstrated that the best way to take in new ideas is when those ideas are presented with the right combination of facts and emotions. Too much of one or too much of the other is ineffective and could make matters worse. We need to find that place where we're emotionally challenged and engaged, but not so provoked as to be massively offended, put off or re-traumatized. One useful rule is that if the emotions get too high, look at the concrete framework and bring the discussion back into the cognitive arena. If it becomes too intellectual, bring in some feelings and imaginings.

The way things are now, we can't get to places where these problems can be appropriately addressed because the questions themselves are too triggering. If one side can pose a disturbing idea in more sensitive, empathic ways and the other side can work on regulating their intense emotional reactions to the challenge, we can learn to deepen difficult conversations and make them tolerable. The new, albeit long and difficult dialogues that will emerge from that space can lead to new solutions to seemingly intractable conflicts and seemingly unsolvable problems.

Our children could probably do these exercises more easily than adults because most of them won't have the same history, the same entrenched ideas and the same triggers. But first they need to be taught the need for emotional problem solving and a methodology for solving them, rather than simply "expressing opinions" about impossibly complex subjects.

Human Understanding IS Rocket Science. It has to be taught in an equally complex trajectory before we can trust our opinions about it. We don't have "opinions" about aerospace engineering unless we're aerospace engineers. Why should it be different with human understanding?

Section IV
The Origins

14

How I Came to Know
What I Know

You might be thinking, this sounds intriguing but very complicated. It would take a massive social movement to implement it. In our evidence-based society, there's no hard data for what I'm proposing. I'm nobody special, yet I'm asking you, individually and collectively, to put the pieces of a puzzle together in a new way and take a massive leap of imagination and faith.

I want this book to catalyze the kind of change that Darwin's book did. *The Origin of Species* changed humankind's consciousness about the existence and nature of evolution. I want to change humankind's consciousness by convincing you that our species must catalyze the next evolutionary leap ourselves, consciously and deliberately.

Why am I the person to initiate this? Why should you believe me? How did I arrive at this, and why should my story be the one that catches hold and catalyzes massive societal change? Who do I think I am?

Because of who I am and how I came to be—the combination of an accident of birth, early childhood experiences, my unusual thinking style and my winding road through psychoanalysis—I came to understand something that other people don't. A simple insight about myself led to insight about the nature of language, the nature of war, the nature of genius, and the reason why "sapiens" is losing its capacity for wisdom. Eventually I tested my hypothesis in a war of ideology that could not be aborted. I did it effectively, in a way that allowed both sides to win, survive and thrive.

I have a theory, and I have a proof of that theory. It's very personal and very complicated, and it involves references to a psychoanalytic process that most of you will know nothing about. Please bear with me while I try to explain.

My story begins in the early 1980s. During my seven and a half year, five days a week personal analysis, the dynamic of creativity emerged. I played with ideas in my own way, but I felt very anxious in classes as I tried to integrate my imagination with the theories and techniques that were being taught to me. One of the core interpretations my analyst made to me was, "You long to be able to think like other people, even though you might be gifted." I freaked out when he said it, but after a while I put it aside and continued.

I loved Freud's model of the unconscious mind with its fantasies, drives, defenses, conflicts and dreams. That seemed right and wonderful to me. But something else didn't feel right. We read the Standard Edition of the Complete Psychological Works of Sigmund Freud and we read the biographies of artists, but it seemed to me that psychoanalysis did not understand creativity at all. Freud's classic line, "Beside the problem of the creative artist psychoanalysis must, alas, lay down its arms," disturbed me more than it did my colleagues. I thought that Freud was playing in a very creative way, making up words, changing his mind whenever new information arose, and writing theoretical love letters to his best friend in an intimate partnership that can be seen in the biography of many great artists. But he saw himself as a scientist, not an artist. He analyzed other personal dynamics in great detail, but he did not examine, or even begin to question, the nature and origin of his own creative genius. It seemed to me that he was laying down his arms against an understanding of creators and creativity, and my teachers accepted that defense.

In Freud's pseudo-scientific model, the goal of the process was the capacity to mourn. You couldn't possess and murder your parents or make your dreams into reality in any concrete way; you could only desire it and sublimate your passions. But it seemed to me that creativity wasn't about mourning. It was about "going for the gold," merging with and "murdering" older models. But there was no theory or methodology addressing the psychological differences between the process of mourning and the process of creative transcendence.

Simply put, Freud's children couldn't leap forward without devaluing him and fragmenting. Einstein could lay Newton to rest in a beautiful coffin. That wasn't happening with Freud.

(Readers immersed in psychoanalysis will argue that much has been written about creativity since that time. My response is that those models are partially accurate and partially defensive. Because we don't have the tools to make genuine creative leaps, psychoanalysis is fracturing rather than effectively transcending its past.)

As I approached graduation, these ideas were swimming around in the back of my unconscious. Consciously I was in full time private practice, a "good girl" at the institute, in the process of terminating analysis and pregnant with my second child. (*What do women want?* Freud pondered without ever answering. *Babies! I responded. Creativity and fertility, duh!*)

Five months into the pregnancy, two weeks before the planned termination date of my analysis, I felt a funny feeling that made me think I might be going into premature labor. The doctor said no, there was nothing on the monitor and I was just nervous. My analyst was a long subway ride from the upper west side to the lower east, an exhausting trip at 7 am. I chose to trust my instincts rather than the doctors and their machines, and I put myself on best rest. After seven and a half years of daily visits, I missed my final two weeks of analysis.

Later I realized that that decision represented a choice between my creative/fertile/feminine side and my analytic side. I chose the former, and that choice delayed the delivery by one lifesaving month. My son was born at 28 weeks instead of 24.

I completed my last two weeks a couple of months later, just before my son was released from the hospital. I associated to the ending as if it had been one of the recurrent almost-dead-baby dreams with which I had started treatment. In those dreams a baby, in many different settings, almost died but didn't. I associated to the miscarriage my mother suffered two weeks before I began school at the age of five, an event I was never told about but reconstructed during analysis.

After that experience and a healthy baby, I was left with a set of fascinating questions. *WTF did I just do?!* It was as if my body had enacted something creatively and even brilliantly, down to the two-week time frame, despite the dynamics being totally outside of conscious awareness. I came to call that kind of enactment "performance art."

In psychoanalysis there was no such thing as "performance art." There was language (good) or there was acting out (bad). They referred to the "primacy of language," but what I had done was dramatically different. It was a kind of visceral, physical "drama."

My analyst closed his practice and retired within a few weeks, and I was left to process the experience with my advisor and three supervisors. Their reactions were disturbingly different, and I felt very confused. *What had just happened, and why are their reactions making me feel worse?!*

Eventually I had an insight. In a true eureka moment, I reconstructed a preverbal experience in a way that would change the direction of my life.

When I was six months old, my wonderful mother was hospitalized for a month with acute pancreatitis that was misdiagnosed as gallbladder disease leading to unnecessary and complicated surgery. My father was at the hospital or working, so I was left in the care of her mother and her three sisters who lived in the same building. The intense feelings I was having as I struggled to make sense of the experience with my supervisors helped me imagine what it must feel like to be an infant, pre-language, when your mother suddenly disappears and you're left with four women that look and feel like her, but definitely are not her. They're not attached to you in the same way, you're not attached to them, and each of them responds to you in a way that is similar and different, loving and unloving, intuiting what you need, and not, at the same time. When you're six months old, you feel a kind of desperation for which no words exist.

On that day, it dawned on me that **my unconscious mind was enacting that preverbal experience in minute detail.** I call that my Helen Keller Moment, because the insight came to me in the shower and it felt like I had just discovered language.

I wrote a paper about my analysis of that experience that I titled, *Creativity: A Work in Progress.* It was published in the *Psychoanalytic Quarterly* in 1993, and it got a prestigious award.

Here's how I described the aftermath of that insight:

At this point one might anticipate that a response would be to stop the behavior and mourn the lost analyst, or if conflicts persisted, to seek out another. But what I experienced was different. It was a feeling not of "Where is he?" but of "THERE he is!" At that moment I felt that I had found the answer for which I had been desperately searching—an understanding of how I thought, a flood of connections to my past, a conviction that I had the capacity for self-analysis and a sense of what the creative process was. The realization that I had been searching for my analyst coincided with the moment of re-finding him—in fact, a better "him." I had ripped my supervisors apart, using any libidinal mechanism I was invited to use, until I had put enough pieces together to resurrect him from the ashes. The associations were to my mother's month-long hospitalization during my first year of life, when I was left in the care of her mother and three sisters, as well as to other losses later in my childhood. For the first time I felt that I could comprehend what an infant might need to do in order to hold on to a memory of her mother for that interminable length of time, and how a positive sense of "self" might be a tentative outcome when she actually returned.

The feelings I was having with my supervisors were the feelings of that baby, a baby who had lost her mother prematurely and was left with relative strangers; people who were trying to give her what she needed but couldn't. What I wanted from my supervisors was an understanding of something that was going on inside of me, something would help me stabilize myself. In that eureka moment I got what I needed. But I didn't get it from them. I got what I needed from myself.

I've always been able to "feed" myself in a way that other people can't. It took me forever to figure that out.

A quarter century later, my hypothesis is that I symbolize differently. When I was eventually given the word "mother," it wasn't just a word to describe and define Peggy Lombardo, the woman who gave birth to me and who loved me more than anyone. For me, the word *mother* was associated with another wordless concept, a quotation-mark "mother," a constellation that represented Grandma, Aunt Helen, Aunt Julia, Aunt Jo and the question that drove me throughout my life, *WTF is a mother?!*

That dynamic constellation—mother, "mother," and WTF is a mother?!— existed in my psyche, and no one ever gave me a word for it because no one understood that "it" was there.

I loved that question more than anything, because I answered it when I was seven months old, and answering it (in an infantile, pre-verbal way) kept me alive and happy. The inaccurate, verbal version might be this: *Wow! There she is! She's like those other people but she's not them. She can go away and come back, and I can remember her by comparing and contrasting her with them. Now I get it!*

I wanted a word for that experience. I was driven by that longing, unconsciously but desperately, throughout my life. Other people may be driven by longings for love or sex or attention or money or a zillion other things. I was driven by the longing for a word, a word that would accurately frame my lived experience and my unusual way of thinking. "Mommy" = my birth mother = Peggy Lombardo wasn't right. That equation may work perfectly for most other people, but for me the word "mother" was more complex than that.

My analyst's interpretation, "You long to be able to think like other people, even though you might be gifted," was as close as anyone could get to imagining that constellation. He couldn't see or label it himself, but he could appreciate that I thought differently from other people, that I saw something no one else could see.

77

My mother—did I tell you she was wonderful?—intuited the same thing. She once said to me, "You know, you were always the perfect child. You did everything you were supposed to do, everything we taught you to do. But it never seemed like you were *from* us. We could *see* you, but we couldn't *imagine* you."

Like my analyst, she understood what she didn't understand and she found ways to communicate that to me. That gift kept me from becoming discouraged, and it kept the pathway for searching open to me.

There's a vast difference between *no one understands me and they never will,* and *no one understands, but they understand that they don't understand so the possibility of one day being understood exists.* One is life-killing, the other life-affirming. Keep that in mind as you try to understand others and be understood by them. **You don't have to pretend to understand, you just have to communicate that they're potentially understandable and worth making the effort.**

My earliest memory appears to confirm this interpretation. When I was a baby, I had a yellow blanket. It's what analysts call a "transitional object," given life by the baby as a way of bridging the divide between self and other. The baby loves that teddy bear or blanket and uses it for soothing en route to separation and sleep. In my memory, my mother covered my blanket with a silky material because it was dirty, and that ruined it for me.

Fast-forward 30 years. When my first son was born, my mother gave him the gift of that blanket, raggedy and definitely not covered. My memory was the exact opposite of what actually occurred. Not only had she not covered it and ruined it for me, she had intuited its importance and saved if for me for 30 years!

Analysis over the course of decades revealed that the "cover" she put over that blanket was language itself. When I learned the word "blanket," I came to understand that it was just a piece of cloth, not a beloved life-giving thing. *Sigh...can't love that anymore....*

I never liked words. I was pretty good at using them, but words forced me to frame things in ways that didn't feel right to me. The need for accuracy in verbal language pulled me away from the creative space that I saw so clearly and gravitated toward, that space where the literal mother and the metaphorical "mother" could dance together. My blanket had represented that space.

In another early memory, I mislabeled a leaf and a flower. I'm not sure which one I mistook for the other, but I was old enough to be embarrassed by the mistake. Over time I came to realize that these word-symbols represented male and female genitals and the definition of masculinity and femininity. Once again, I resisted labeling them because I didn't like the distinctions society was offering me.

I still don't. Ask me to define "man" and "woman" and I'll go to my imaginary playground, work to solve the fascinating question, and emerge a decade later with a picture that feels right to me. Ask me to define them in a Wikipedia-like, socially and linguistically accurate way, and I'll be stymied.

15

Why am I Telling You This Story?

I want you to understand the thing that I do, because I want to teach you how to do it.

It's not intuitive for other people the way it is for me, but it's a methodology that's teachable. *If you're faced with an unsolvable problem, put it aside. Move it to a different arena and play with it there, ideally with other people*. If the people that you long to respond to you aren't able to give you what you need, don't mourn or get angry and discouraged. Find the equivalent of Grandma and the Aunts and struggle to get what you want in that alternate arena. Translate new insights back into the verbal arena using language, metaphor or art.

For example, if you're religious and someone else says, "Religion is stupid," it will feel as if your beloved God/parent/blanket, and the space of comfort and meaning it offers is being pulled out from under you. Instead of fighting or fleeing, instead of mourning the loss of your friendship or directly confronting that person, use this new technique. Find another space to think and to play, a space where paradoxical ideas are interesting and worthy of exploration. Learn to be curious.

Speaking of regulation of powerful emotions, I should tell you that my superpower is the same as my kryptonite. I have a lot of trouble feeling sad.

I often wonder, if the word "sadness" and the expression of it didn't exist all around me, whether I would have discovered it myself.

When I'm threatened with loss, I won't get depressed and I won't get mad at the world or mad at God or mad at the entity that took it away. I will search desperately, and eventually effectively, until I re-find that object in another arena and translate it back using metaphor. Sadness, interrupted.

The Jewish and Palestinian people can do this. Liberals and conservatives can do it. Religious people and atheists can do it. It won't be as natural for you as it is for me, but it's a teachable trick. Once you master it, you won't have to feel profoundly sad or terribly destabilized if your strongly-held beliefs are challenged. If you learn to play well with others in an imaginary sandbox, you can find new and even more satisfying answers without losing your personal center.

How can we actively engage with people who misunderstand, ridicule or hate us? By going to the good people in the other group and asking, genuinely, *Why don't you like me?* No matter how painful or off-putting the responses are, it's essential that you listen attentively to honest answers and remain in dialogue over a long period of time.

We all tend to ward off potentially painful challenges—painful because they're wrong or painful because they're right—by repeating mantras about how bad being "anti" is. I don't like words that end in "ism" or "phobia." Racism, sexism, anti-Semitism, homophobia, Islamophobia…the use of those words makes people feel defensive and invites a "fight or flight" response. *I get the feeling that you don't like me or you don't feel comfortable around people like me* works a lot better, especially if you can tolerate the response of, *Yes, you're right, I don't.* If you do that, you will open up a pathway and a playground rather than create a barrier.

Feeling hurt, misunderstood and offended is a loss. It leads to hard-to-tolerate emotions, and even loss of the ability to think. The desire to retaliate and show the other side what it feels like is human and powerful. But all that does is lead to solidification of barriers and the development of bigger and better weapons.

You know that symbol I longed to have, a word to represent the space where my metaphorical, quotation-mark "mother" lived? That word would be *so* useful for humankind! **Calling it a "pathway" or a "playground" would normalize the experience and make it a more inviting place to enter.**

Think of the people in that playground as analogous to the people in my family who took me in but didn't love me the way my own family did. If you enter that space with people who are different from you, you're going to ask, *WTF is going on! I don't like this! I want what I'm used to!* over and over and over.

Relax into it. Realize that they come from a different center and they're not wired to "get" you. They see the world differently. That's human, and it's okay. Try not to feel hurt by their misunderstanding. Realize that you're misunderstanding them too. If you keep at it, you'll get better at the language of that very human "dance." A light bulb will go off eventually and you'll understand something in a new way. So, maybe, will they.

Once good, thoughtful people can learn to solve problems together, one of the problems they'll solve is how to deal with extremists. There will always be people who can't learn and can't play well with others, people who lack a conscience or are so traumatized that nothing will help. There will always be prisons and people who kill. But eventually those people will become singularities, not given license to rise to the surface and hold the rest of society hostage. We can make that happen.

16

I Fought a War
and We Both Won

Seriously, I did that. A couple decades ago, after the experience I described, I went to see the person I considered to be the best analyst around. To me he represented the best and the worst in the field as it existed at that time.

When I wrote that paper, I understood that I had essentially changed psychoanalytic theory around my own experience. I had reframed the problem of creativity in a way that had massive implications—not just for me, but for my field.

The responses I got were at once wonderful and defensive. I got applause, presentations, publication in my favorite journal and a prestigious, rarely-given award given to a young analyst who contributed something new to analytic theory. I heard, "Great paper, Alice. Congratulations!" over and over. I felt like I had just announced that the earth revolved around the sun rather than the sun around the earth, and the response was, "That's really a great paper," with no attempt to wrap their minds around the meaning and potential impact.

There was now a significant dissonance between my way of thinking and the thinking of the analysts in my community, to the point where I wasn't sure how to do the work I had been taught to do in the way I had been taught to do it. Whose problem was it, and what could be done about it?

I went to Dr. X with that problem. I told him that I was having a flood of new ideas, and I didn't know what to do with them given that the good people around me had their understandably entrenched ways of thinking and working. I didn't want to start another analytic sect; there were enough of them popping up already. I wanted to search for a greater truth.

In that first meeting, as I talked about having a flood of new ideas, I referenced a friend of his that was quoted in a newsletter we had both received that day. The quote was something like this: "With the exception of a genius like Freud, the average individual has no more than one original idea in his lifetime, possibly (probably?) none." He responded by reassuring me that that wasn't true, that a person could have a lot of new ideas without being a genius like Freud.

That was supposed to be reassuring, but it wasn't. We ended saying that we would both think about the problem and perhaps get together at a later time.

I walked away with a powerful and scary realization.

I had just gotten my first-ever laptop, so I sat down to write him a letter. I explained that I found his comment to be the opposite of reassuring. I didn't want him to argue against that statement about genius, because I agreed with it.

As I wrote that letter, I realized something. I realized that I had grown up with the fantasy of myself as a genius. I had struggled for decades to suppress that fantasy, and later to analyze it away as a permutation of some kind of hideous narcissism.

For the first time, I considered the possibility that perhaps I had been wrong to assume it was a pathological fantasy. For the first time, I considered the possibility that maybe I was, or had the potential to be, a great mind.

A few weeks later I met him in the hallway. He said, very simply, "You'll have to prove it." I thought I had died and gone to heaven.

He didn't confirm or refute my imagining; it would have been inappropriate if he had. What he did was open up a space; that play space that I had been unconsciously longing for. *Can I go there? Can I really go there?! Will you play with me in that space?*

We met again, and I asked him if we could co-create an inside-out permutation of psychoanalysis that I came to call "catalysis." Instead of meeting five times a week with money changing hands, we would meet five times a year free of charge and he would read letters that I would write between meetings. The process would not be about one person analyzing the psychological defects of another. It would be about the problem of difference and a shared search for truth.

I have 14 years of theoretical/philosophical love letters in my file cabinet and floppy disks, if anyone ever wants to read them.

The first decade was wonderful. The dynamic tension, along with the opportunity for massive flights of imagination that I could document in letters (mostly from me, but sometimes from him), was exactly what I needed. When we met we would sometimes talk about the letters, but often we wouldn't. Sometimes we would talk about personal things, or literature, analytic theory, events in the news, the movies. Sometimes we would get really mad at each other. I'd process the experience in the snail-mail letters that I wrote every couple of weeks, give or take.

I settled into a Clark Kent kind of life. I told a few close friends, but I soon learned that what I was doing was impossible to describe accurately. (You can imagine the distortions, right?) I learned to master my superpowers in secret and all was well.

You might think that this would end well. I was figuring stuff out, he was cooperating beautifully in the attempt, and we both lived our separate lives and did our separate work. Cool.

No, not cool. I know how ideological differences lead to war, because we were eventually compelled to fight one. We were two smart, wonderful, well-intentioned people who cared about each other a lot, and yet we were drawn into a year-long battle that had every element of war but the bloodshed. It was a war that I predicted in the letters, yet it was impossible to prevent.

Here's how it happened:

For me, the play space that we had co-created needed to be a Thing—a thing with a name and a definition and a methodology. If *psychoanalysis* was a process with a name and a definition and a methodology, why couldn't *catalysis* be a similar kind of process?

In the beginning was the Word, and the Word was with God, and the Word was God. (John 1:1).

I wanted to give birth to our baby, name it "Catalysis," and describe it for the outside world in a way that would invite them to reach for it, play with it and eventually imitate it. I desperately wanted a Word, a word that would make our playground real and give it life beyond what it was. To the extent that Dr. X was my transference God, I needed a Word to attach to him and to our process, a Word that would be The Beginning of a new organic creation.

But he didn't see the thing that I saw in the way that I saw it. What he saw was that he was a friend who was doing me a favor and helping me figure stuff out. In his world, when people figured stuff out they wrote papers about the stuff they figured out, and the people who supported them in the attempt were not referenced. I had been there and done that. From my perspective, giving birth to analytic papers was like giving birth to a stillborn baby. I wasn't going to go there again. I was going to give birth to a new life force, a dynamic change process, not disembodied ideas that would be dead on arrival.

From my vantage point, he and I were doing something original and wonderful. We had co-created a new space, a space for the analysis of difference rather than defect, a space that other people could see and imitate and write about and benefit from. There were precedents all over the art world. Artists typically have patrons, mentors, teachers, coaches, lovers, siblings, editors, friends, spouses, partners, and other kinds of "secret sharers" to love and hate and merge with and separate from en route to discovery. Psychoanalysis emerged from Freud's theoretical/philosophical love letters to his best friend Wilhelm Fliess. Dr. X knew that, didn't he?

After a decade, I was desperate for our co-created process to emerge into the light of day. But because he couldn't see the shape that I saw, he experienced my desire as a fantasy that I needed to analyze so I could make it go away. In his world, analysts were expected to be anonymous. Patients couldn't know anything about you; it would interfere with the development of transference fantasies and could ruin the process. In his world, talking behind someone's back was considered a boundary violation, something that was morally and ethically wrong. Besides, if we talked about each other, our perspectives would be different and the people in our community would easily misinterpret our decade-long process. He had been bending the rules in a way that could be misinterpreted as an "acting out" on his part, and that was a mortal sin in his world. (Did I tell you that we kissed goodbye at the end of each session, just a peck on the cheek like a father saying goodbye to a daughter? If they thought he was trying to be some kind of therapist for me, he could get excommunicated for that.)

We were stuck. Maneuvers were made here and there, but we couldn't effectively escape from the trap. Both of us were invested in a search for truth and meaning, but after awhile that was no longer the primary fuel source. He was less invested in the process than I was, but he understood that opting out wasn't an option. If he tried to stop me by cutting me off, I could "kill" him, and he knew it.

We were at an ideological dead end. Neither of us was going to budge. If I talked I could make him look really bad, and he would deny or reframe it in a way that would make me look really bad. There was no place for compromise. We were going to kill each other.

17

We Were Going to
Kill Each Other...

... $\bigcup$ntil I came up with a idea.

In August of 2001, I wrote the first chapter of a book. It revealed, from my perspective, what he and I were doing and what the problem was in talking about it. I worked on it until it was beautifully written, and I shared it with him and with some of the analysts in our community.

He freaked, they freaked, I freaked. It was horrifying and confusing, heartfelt and beautiful, aggressive and challenging, at the same time. If I had tried to talk about it I would have looked like a babbling fool. The creativity made it compelling.

For a year, he moved one way, they moved another way, and I wrote another chapter based on my understanding of what was happening at that moment. A month after that first letter 9/11 happened, and that dynamic got integrated into the story as well. It was a hideous experience for both of us, but writing the book in real time kept the pathway open and prevented mutual annihilation. We met less often, but we still met.

It was awful until the last session, the one we decided—he decided—would end it. That was as perfect as the rest was terrible. By the end of that hour a shared insight emerged that allowed both of us to transition from confusion to insight, misery to joy. And we both lived happily ever after.

Seriously, we did. The war ended in a way that allowed both of us to survive and thrive. It felt like Hamlet with a happy ending.

It's going to be hard to explain. I'll try my best.

At the very last moment, he said something that was typical of him, something well-intentioned but missing me. You know how I think in this weirdly abstract, shape-shifting, metaphorical, cross-modalities way, right? You know those thinking style differences I shared with you in Section 2? That's the place where we were most different, so it was the place where we came into head-on collision. I wish I could remember exactly what was said, but I don't. Whatever it was, I felt massively frustrated, and I responded with, "*God, you're concrete!*"

He replied, with obvious sadness, "You're right, I am. See? I'm a disappointment to you."

At the beginning of our work together he had predicted, "I'm going to disappoint you." I replied maybe, but I was willing to take that risk. His prediction was about to come true.

In the psychiatric world, concrete thinking is a problem. If you say that the subway brought you instead of your depression, or that an apple and an orange aren't alike because they look and taste different, or that people shouldn't live in glass houses because the glass will break, you're going to have trouble negotiating the world.

Analytic ideas seemed very abstract and we screened for people who were capable of abstract thinking. But after a while psychoanalysis became more like a religion, so concrete thinking rose to the surface without anybody realizing it. The id, ego and superego, penis envy and castration anxiety, the Oedipus complex, etc. were presented as concrete entities, which drove me crazy because they weren't. He certainly wasn't concrete in the classic sense, but over time his field, which was becoming like a religion, brought that out in him. I must have made him feel like the most concrete person in the world as he struggled to hold on to his thinking style and the dynamic constellations around which his thoughts, his life's work and his self-esteem were organized.

He didn't get me because he didn't get me, because he wasn't capable of getting me. Because neither of us realized this, we hadn't talked about this dynamic at all during our work together.

I had written many letters about thought process and language differences from a theoretical perspective, but that dynamic had never entered the personal arena as a phenomenon that might have interfered with mutual understanding. I needed him to be my "God," so I didn't allow recognition of that simple human difference to become conscious, and he didn't either.

During those last minutes of our last meeting, he felt really, really sad, and—here's the beautiful part—he acknowledged it.

Like I said, sadness isn't in my repertoire. My world was ending, but I didn't feel the same emotion that he did.

That's when I felt that light bulb go off. When he said, *"You're right, I am. See, I'm a disappointment to you,"* I replied, *"That's exactly what I've been trying to tell you!! That's what I mean by a* '*language' difference! The problem between us arose from that simple thinking style difference. Like I've been saying, language differences lead to war!!*"

That turned on his light bulb and it instantly stopped the war. I watched his face transition from sad to happy.

That's it!
We got it, right?!
Yeah, we did.
Wow, how awesome was that?!

We hugged and kissed goodbye for the last time, grinning ear to ear. We had just fought a war that we both won, and we had pulled it off just as the clock was running out.

You had to be there to fully appreciate it, but maybe the movie version will get it right.

18
Separation and Forward Movement

Because we parted with insight and affection rather than the sense of an impossible divide that could only be resolved through mutually assured destruction, a new pathway quickly opened up for me. It was a long one, but it was staring me in the face and I knew I would have the confidence to negotiate it. I had imagined a theory about the way ideological and thought process differences lead to war, tested that hypothesis in vivo, and my hypothesis proved to be correct.

Now I had a potential new product, not just an idea. All I needed to do was find a way to market that product to the world in a way that would be effective. It was a daunting task, but not impossible. I finished the real-time book and put it in my file cabinet to save for release at the appropriate time, probably after his death and maybe mine.

I had been writing about the importance of the time dimension for years, so I knew I would have to wait patiently for time to tame the emotions, allow for synthesis and healing, and open new pathways. As much as I longed to show him how much he had done for me and maybe the world, I understood that it would only be possible for Moses to glimpse the Promised Land.

Meanwhile, I found other people to play with and went on to develop new projects in new playgrounds. Take a look at these websites:

www.changingourconsciousness.org - my non-profit organization/blog

www.emotionalimprint.org - the education project described in Section 2

www.thehotstoveproject.org - the mental health project and documentaries that I co-created with Dr. Lois Oppenheim

www.divides.org - the e-book that my students wrote based on the work of Dr. Volkan

If you go to these links, you'll see that I've been pulling my ideas together while working in transitional arenas midway between older paradigms and my newer one. At the same time, I've been setting the stage for a leap into the public arena. Dr. X, my catalytic partner, was replaced by the wonderful colleagues who helped me co-create these projects.

These catalytic partnerships came to include the 400-something friends on my personal Facebook page and the 900-something friends on my public page, the Depth Perception Party. For several years I've been posting every morning in both of those arenas. I work hard to coax people of different cultures, ages, religions, education levels, careers and political positions to talk to, rather than at, about and against one another. In those spaces I bring my ideas alive, demonstrating how hard it is to talk across divides and how important it is to make the effort.

Recently some members of my Facebook groups took the risk of trying online dialogue projects of their own. They wrote about the outcomes of their attempts to catalyze dialogue across ideological divides in an unpublished paper titled, *Talking Across Divides: The Paper Airplane Project*. They saw how hard it was, and how possible it might one day be. If Human Understanding is Rocket Science, all we could do at this point was build paper airplanes and see how long we could keep them up.

I've spent much time working with young people because they're the ones who will have to take these simple ideas, make them their own, and take them to new places. I've also spent time with people struggling with psychotic disorders. Both groups have much to teach us.

I've been preparing to enter the public arena, where I expect, once again, to embrace powerful reactions en route to making my vision into reality. This book represents my transition to that arena.

19
Genius

Genius. That's such a forbidden word, isn't it? We use it liberally in all the wrong ways (*My son got all A's again; he's such a genius! That's a genius breakfast cereal!*), but we only have vague ideas, more descriptive than explanatory, about how people like Da Vinci, Shakespeare and Einstein thought. Because we don't understand that dynamic constellation as it exists in its primitive forms, we can't recognize signs and we can't provide appropriate environments to nurture it. As a result, genius hasn't been able to rise up in the humanistic arenas. Science and technology develop rapidly because the best minds are allowed to rise to the top. But the world is run by compromised people, not visionary leaders.

Individual people are encouraged to be honest about other parts of their self-representation. *I'm on the autistic spectrum. I have a learning disability. I got accepted to Harvard.* But if we say, *I think I may be a genius or have the potential to be one,* there's no nurturing environment, no soil that will allow that mutant seedling to survive and thrive. If you speak those words in any way at any time, even as a fantasy, you will horrify people. You'll instantly be labeled grandiose and narcissistic, and you'll be pressured to shut up and be humble. You'll be told you don't deserve that label until you produce something great. But how can an individual person produce something great without a nurturing environment and the contributions of others? The Wright Brothers could build the first airplane themselves. In the 21st century, no one could build a spaceship to Mars herself, no matter how visionary the model might be.

Genius is a thing, not a desire to show off. But if we can't recognize that dynamic constellation, if we refuse to look for it and push it away when it asks to be recognized, we won't ever be able to nurture potentiality in the human arenas. So many potential great minds may be out there, living compromised lives because compromise is all that's available to them. I had to hijack my own creative partner and demand the creation of the nurturing environment that I knew I needed. Lots of other factors gave me the confidence and the ability to create that matrix for myself, but most potential geniuses don't win the nurturing lottery and the just-plain-luck lottery at the same time.

I think the difference between genius and brilliance has to do with the way people symbolize, but so far I just have an n of 1. I hope that one of the outcomes of this short presentation is that your minds will be open to the possibility that more people like me exist, and we deserve recognition, definition, nurturing, appropriate challenge, and an accurate word to define us.

Or maybe that will turn out not to be true. Maybe the identifying factor is that the factors can't be identified. We should figure that out if it's true.

Epilogue

You know why we can't solve the problem of war? Because we try too hard to make the leap from war to peace, offering little more than bad compromises in between. People aren't going to do that. It's not human nature to want to do that, or to be able to do that. It's human nature to sacrifice our lives before we will sacrifice our identities and our beliefs. Our identities and our beliefs ARE our lives.

There's an epidemic of cutting in young people. Physical pain helps, because it centers the existential emotional pain, the pain that can't be spoken about and relieved. The pain and the blood are real. They serve as a distraction from the wordless and more agonizing pain that comes from being chronically misunderstood and unheard.

That happens on a large scale too. After 9/11, we needed to come together around a shared enemy. We needed to feel the real pain of war, because the pain of asking, *Who are these people and why do they hate us so much?* and living within that uncomfortable space for the time needed to gain deeper insight into the problem, seemed intolerable.

When events like that happen, the solution won't come from one extremist fighting with another extremist while good people demand compromises that both sides refuse to accept. The solution will come from the good people in the middle coming together and creating a space where they're free to ask, *Why don't you like us?* The solution will come when they can listen attentively to the answer and try to understand without instinctively and defensively arguing back.

That process will hurt. A lot. You'll get angry and defensive; they'll get angry and defensive. You'll misunderstand, and you'll be misunderstood in an equally powerful way. You'll come up against thought process differences, ideological differences, individual and group defenses, problems with self-esteem regulation, and personal triggers from past traumas. One person will attribute a phenomenon to God while the other will think that's a crazy idea. Money, because it's real and symbolic at the same time, will figure significantly. In individual relationships, opposites attract and opposites repel. The same is true on the world stage.

Talking together over time, asking challenging questions, listening to the painful reasons why people dislike you and/or your large group, making sense of thinking style differences, fighting powerful battles and seeing how yours compare with the ones on the wider stage...all of that will be necessary.

We can't avoid war because we can't avoid conflict. We need conflict to become separate and distinct individuals. We like conflict; without it life is too boring. But we can discover ways to fight conflicts in words and resolve them, or at least tame the feelings until time intervenes. We can do that using a methodology that can be developed, taught and practiced. That methodology will allow everyone to feel understood, tolerate mourning the parts of their beliefs that are no longer valid, and enable new and overarching truths to rise to the surface. Religious people, atheists and scientists can search together for more complex answers to why we're here, where we came from and where we're going. If God lies at Infinity we may never arrive at a final answer, but we can move beyond the place where we're presently stuck and discover a shared excitement about new questions, new hypotheses and new meanings.

We don't even have to lay down our computers to do this, as long as we keep in mind that real human beings reside on the other side of the screen.

About the Author

Alice Lombardo Maher, M.D. is a graduate of the Albert Einstein College of Medicine and the Institute for Psychoanalytic Education at NYU School of Medicine. She is the Founder and Director of Changing Our Consciousness (changingourconsciousness.org), a non-profit organization dedicated to emotional literacy and dialogue across ideological divides. COC's education project, Emotional Imprint™ (emotionalimprint.org), is developing a K-12 curriculum aiming to incorporate a new language for understanding and responding to the emotional communications of others.

Dr. Maher also co-created The Hot Stove Project (thehot-stoveproject.org), a comprehensive set of resources dedicated to the greater social integration of people who think, feel or behave outside of expected norms.

Dr. Maher practices psychiatry and psychoanalysis in New York City.

CPSIA information can be obtained
at www.ICGtesting.com
Printed in the USA
BVHW041352270120
570620BV00017B/1644